P9-AZW-823

THE 101 BEST

Tropical Fishes

THE ADVENTUROUS AQUARIST™ GUIDE SERIES

Produced and distributed by:

T.F.H. Publications, Inc.
One T.F.H. Plaza
Third and Union Avenues
Neptune City, NJ 07753
www.tfh.com

Printed and bound in China
09 10 11 12 13   3 5 7 9 8 6 4

ISBN-13: 978-1-890087-93-7
ISBN-10: 1-890087-93-9
UPC-A: 6-81290-08793-5

Library of Congress Cataloging-in-Publication Data
Wood, Kathleen.
The 101 best tropical fishes : how to choose & keep hardy, brilliant, fascinating species that will thrive in your home aquarium / by Kathleen Wood; with Mary E. Sweeney and Scott W. Michael.
p. cm. -- (The adventurous aquarist(tm) guide)
Includes bibliographical references and index.
ISBN 1-890087-93-9 (alk. paper)
1. Tropical fish. 2. Aquariums. I. Sweeney, Mary Ellen. II. Michael, Scott W. III. Title.
SF457.W66 2007
639.34'2--dc22   2008028294

Color by Digital Engine
Designed by Linda Provost

A MICROCOSM/TFH Professional Series Book

TFH Publications, Inc.
Neptune City, NJ 07753
www.tfh.com

Microcosm, Ltd.
Charlotte, VT 05445
www.microcosm-books.com

THE 101 BEST

Tropical Fishes

HOW TO CHOOSE & KEEP HARDY, BRILLIANT, FASCINATING SPECIES THAT WILL THRIVE IN YOUR HOME AQUARIUM

by Kathleen Wood
with
Mary E. Sweeney
and Scott W. Michael

MICROCOSM

tfh

PROFESSIONAL
SERIES™

THE ADVENTUROUS AQUARIST™ GUIDE SERIES

A MICROCOSM EDITION

WWW.MICROCOSMAQUARIUMEXPLORER.COM

Cover Photographs

Blue Gourami (*Trichogaster trichopterus*), page 98; TFH Archives

Back Cover

Top: Ram Cichlid (*Microgeophagus ramirezi*), page 87; TFH Archives
Middle: Rummynose Tetra (*Hemigrammus bleheri*), page 138; TFH Archives
Bottom: Clown Loach (*Chromobotia macracanthus*), page 111; TFH Archives

Spine

Cardinal Tetra (*Paracheirodon axelrodi*), page 132; TFH Archives

To a truly remarkable aquarist

and good "fishy" friend, Alfred D. Castro.

He helped me learn from my mistakes and never give

up, and showed me that there are few problems so

great that they can't be solved by

a partial water change.

He is greatly missed.

ACKNOWLEDGEMENTS

This book would not have been possible without the assistance of a number of people who I've had the pleasure of getting to know over the years, both through my involvement in the aquarium hobby and by working on a number of marine and freshwater publications. My thanks to Scott Michael for demonstrating that he is not only an excellent marine aquarist and underwater photographer, but is also quite adept at things freshwater by penning the "Stocking your Aquarium" section for this book. Likewise, my appreciation to Wayne Leibel for allowing me to tap into his vast knowledge of Central and South American cichlids. Thanks as well to Dr. Ronald Shimek for giving me the benefit of his editorial "eye." I am indebted to Lee Finley for providing me with a variety of excellent references, including a wonderful original copy of William T. Innes' *Exotic Aquarium Fishes*.

I appreciate all the hard work put forth by the team at Microcosm, including editor Mary Sweeney, designers extraordinaire Susie Forbes and Linda Provost, editors Alesia Depot, Judith Billard, John Sweeney, Janice Heilmann, and editor & publisher James Lawrence. Photographer and friend, Aaron Norman, was a great help in providing many of the beautiful images, often at a moment's notice, and Ryan Greene at T.F.H. did yeoman service in assembling hundreds of brilliant photographs.

Thanks also to the aquarium professionals from New England to Nebraska to Southern California who helped in the vexatious task of winnowing down the species lists, especially aquarium shop owners and managers Tyler and Madeleine Dawson and Jason Boczar at The Pet Advantage and Gerry Hine at Green Mountain Aquarium.

And finally, thank you to my two English Bulldogs, Marilyn and Luke, and Katie, the Lab who came to visit and never left, for sacrificing their daily jaunts to the Dog Park so that I might complete this book. All I can say is, "I owe you big time!"

—Kathleen A. Wood
Laguna Beach, California

CONTENTS

Silver Hatchetfish (Gasteropelecus sternicla), page 109.

CONTENTS

Meant as a field guide to freshwater aquarium species, this handbook uses color photographs taken in home aquariums and in the wild for quick visual identification. Species appearing here have been selected as outstanding for their hardiness and durability in aquarium conditions, for their attractiveness, interesting behaviors and availability to freshwater enthusiasts.

Fishes are arranged alphabetically by common name within their general or family groupings. General groupings in this book include the Anabantids or Labyrinthfishes, Catfishes and the Livebearers. Old World fishes come from Africa and Asia, New World species from Central and South America.

Subheadings within each species account contain concise reference material, advice and comments organized as follows:

COMMON NAME

At least one common name is listed for each species. Common names with the widest acceptance in the aquarium hobby are used. The first name provided is the name most frequently used in the authoritative checklists and field guides written by ichthyologists. In assigning the preferred common name to each species, we have attempted to steer away from obvious misnomers and toward names that will minimize confusion and bring science and hobby closer together.

SCIENTIFIC NAME

This is the most-current scientific name applied to the fish by the ichthyological community. The name is in the form of a binomial. The first name indicates the genus to which the fish belongs, while the second is the species name—for example, the Clown Loach (*Chromobotia macracanthus*).

MAXIMUM LENGTH

This indicates the greatest length that an individual of that particular species can attain—or the longest ever reported—measuring from the end of the snout to the tip of the tail. In most cases, the length of most aquarium specimens will fall short of this measure, but the aquarist should always plan for the prospect of his or her fish reaching a maximum length close to that presented.

NATIVE RANGE

This entry notes the broad geographical area where each species occurs. The distribution of a fish is of great value to those aquarists wishing to set up a tank that represents a natural community from a certain geographical region.

MINIMUM AQUARIUM SIZE

This is the minimum suitable aquarium volume for an adult individual of the species. Juveniles and adolescents can be housed in smaller tanks. Activity levels and behavior patterns of a particular species have been accounted for whenever possible. Providing as much room as possible results in less stress and reduced aggression among tankmates.

SWIMMING LEVEL

Many aquarium fishes have preferred areas, both in the wild and the aquarium, in which they spend most of their time. There are the bottom dwellers, like many of the catfishes, that rarely, if ever, rise to other areas in the tank; midwater swimmers, such as the barbs and tetras, which typically school in groups in the midwater sections of the aquarium and occasionally visit the other two areas; and top swimmers like bettas and hatchetfishes that spend their time at the surface. Among other things, these designations must be taken into account when feeding certain fishes, such as bottom-dwelling catfishes, as they must be offered special types of foods designed to sink to the bottom or fed when other midwater to top swimmers are less active, to ensure that these fishes receive sufficient nutrition.

FEEDING

Freshwater fishes have a wide range of feeding preferences and requirements. Advice in this section includes the type of foods generally preferred by the species, and how and when to feed them to ensure that fishes at every swimming level in the aquarium receive enough to eat.

Meaty foods include: fresh, frozen and freeze-dried varieties, including mysid (*Mysis*) and brine shrimp (*Artemia*), krill, insect larvae, and worms of various types. A number of prepared frozen foods are specially formulated for cichlids, catfishes, and others.

Live foods include adult or newly hatched brine shrimp (*Artemia*), mysid shrimp (*Mysis*), mosquito larvae, whiteworms, bloodworms and black worms (*Tubifex*).

Herbivore foods range from flaked and frozen preparations that contain unicellular algae (especially *Spirulina*) to table vegetables, such as spinach, zucchini and Romaine lettuce, and even canned vegetables packed in water. These are always rinsed well or blanched before feeding, and typically weighted down with a rubber-band or attached to the glass with a plastic clip sold in most aquarium stores. For bottom-feeding fishes, sinking wafers, sticks, pellets, and tablets can be a godsend.

Color enhancers are now recommended for many freshwater aquarium species. An increasing number of prepared foods contain added vitamins and pigments, such as carotenoids, to help enhance the fishes' natural colors.

HABITAT

Many tropical fishes do best in aquariums aquascaped to replicate the environment they inhabit in the wild. Many need planted tanks to feel at home and thrive; many others only acclimate well when provided with a profusion of rocky caves and hiding places in the tankscape for a sense of security. Many fishes require ample swimming space and prefer tanks with plantings arranged at the back and ends of the aquascape.

BREEDING

This section offers a brief designation of the breeding strategy used by the species being discussed. For example, in the species account for the Glowlight Tetra, It is noted that the species scatters adhesive eggs among fine-leaved plants and requires special water conditions to encourage spawning. For more on the reproductive strategies of various species included, look to the Breeding section beginning on page 178.

A community of mixed angelfishes in a deep tank with a plant-filled aquascape well-suited to the size, temperament and habitat requirements of the species.

Hard-learned lessons: how to pick fishes that will thrive

My entry into the world of fishkeeping was quite by accident and for all the wrong reasons. I was living in a small apartment and needed a divider to separate the kitchen from the living room. A 6-foot aquarium seemed just the thing, and besides, I'd always wanted to keep fish but the time never seemed right. So, I bought a 125-gallon tank and brought it home.

A month later and several hundred dollars poorer, I had my tank up and running...but there it sat, still empty. What to do? I knew next to nothing about fish, so I decided to make the rounds of my local tropical fish stores. There were so many pretty and interesting species to choose from that I found myself overwhelmed. Which ones should I start with and would they all get along? Confused, I finally knew what I was going to do. I'd throw a "fish-tank-warming party." I sent out invitations asking each guest to bring one tropical fish.

For the next week I received calls from most of the stores in the area, each asking me to be more specific about the kinds of fish I was thinking about. Did I want gouramis? How about a knifefish? And on and on. Everyone seemed to be getting involved in this fishy endeavor. By the time party night arrived, I had probably spoken with just about every shop in the area and, by the end of the evening, I was the proud owner of a tank full of around 75 fish (no one brought just one!), from a Ghost Knifefish to tetras to gouramis... you name it, I had it. All types of fishes from all types of habitats from all over the world, all with various and different needs. There I was with a tank full of living, breathing fishes and not a clue what to do next besides sprinkle in some flake food a few times a day. And so began an odyssey into the fascinating world of tropical fishes that has lasted for over 30 years.

ALL THE RIGHT REASONS

One of the great things about the aquarium hobby is that there are so many possibilities. Over the years I've watched the numbers and varieties of wonderful tropical fishes grow to the point that we now have a staggering array to choose from. Walking into the tropical fish section of just about any pet store is like being a kid in a candy store. So many colors and fin types, so little time. But, just because you can, doesn't mean you should.

When I was the editor of *Aquarium Fish Magazine*, I received countless letters and phone calls from frustrated hobbyists who were at their wits' ends and about to throw in the towel. Their fishes were dying, the water cloudy—fishkeeping was just too difficult and not very rewarding. When questioned further, it turned out that many of these newcomers were suffering from the common beginner's ailment of leaping before they looked. They had purchased fishes based on a whim of the moment, with little or no consideration of what would happen once they got the fishes home. Few had bothered to ask: How big would they get? Would all the fish get along? Do I have the right setup for the fish I picked?

No one acquires an aquarium with the intention of failing or of killing fish. In fact, lack of success (and lost fish) is the number-one reason why there are so many empty 10-gallon tanks at garage sales. But, what I've learned over the years is that having a thriving aquarium is not that hard—all it takes is a little thought and planning before you start and whenever you buy a new fish.

This book is designed to make stocking a freshwater aquarium less of a mystery and to give you some tools to get started on the road to success with tropical fishes. This hobby is too much fun for people to end up frustrated because they made bad choices when acquiring their fishes.

We've tried to choose fishes for the Species Accounts that are hardy, easy to keep, attractive and interesting. These are the species we would recommend to a best friend or relative wanting to stock a new aquarium—or restocking more intelligently after an initial failure.

We've also included some up-to-date husbandry guidelines and advice, as well as chapters and practical tips on creating balanced fish communities in tanks of various sizes, on foods and feeding, and choosing healthy fishes. All with the goal of helping you to avoid the mistakes I made when I started in the hobby.

So, what happened to the 75 fish crammed together in my 125-gallon room divider? Luckily, a friendly clerk I encountered on one of my never-ending trips to the pet stores to buy yet another

A classic neophyte mistake: impulse buys of species such as this Bala Shark, only to watch as it grows to 14 in. (40 cm) and eats all your smaller fishes.

medication to solve yet another problem turned out to be a very knowledgable teenage "fish geek." With great patience, he proceeded to guide me out of the morass of troubles I had gotten myself and my fishes into.

During that time I learned which of the 75 were compatible and returned those that were not and which types of fishes were suitable for my setup. Finally, after many returns and lost fish, I had a perfect community of 25 bottom, midwater and top-swimming fishes, many of which I was able to enjoy for years. It would have been so much easier (not to mention less costly) to have done it right in the first place.

The best advice I can give anyone entering or exploring this wonderful hobby is to take your time and buy the right fish for the right reasons.

The Hornet Cichlid (Tilapia buttikoferi): a beautiful West African species, but best suited to large tanks with tankmates of a similar size and temperament.

The art & science of creating a balanced fish community

Scott W. Michael

As if it were yesterday, I can clearly remember walking into a tropical fish store for the first time. Walls of glowing tanks, packed with piscine gems. The place had the warmth, humidity and distinctive aromas of a well-kept aquarium shop, more than slightly suggestive of the exotic tropics. It was sensory overload for a young mind.

Within the tanks was a multitude of shapes, colors and behaviors. Some fishes were dashing about the upper layers of the aquariums. Some were peeking out from behind rocks or weaving in and out of thickets of plants. Others rested on the bottom or adhered to the glass walls of their aquariums.

Within minutes, I had found dozens of fishes that I wanted to take home to keep in my own 10-gallon ecosystem. Fortunately, the store owner was a conscientious fish enthusiast and he gently guided me toward a few hardy fish that would help me establish my new aquarium, fish that would survive as I learned the basics of fishkeeping. He also introduced some concepts that I had never considered: selecting fishes that occupy different "layers" from top to bottom, those that gravitate to different microhabitats within the tank and choosing fishes that perform important tasks in the aquarium, like algae-eating and scavenging uneaten food from the bottom.

A WORLD OF CHOICES

There are literally hundreds of fish species commonly available to the tropical fishkeeper. This amazing selection is often overwhelming to the neophyte. The prudent aquarist will not buy every fish that catches his or her eye, but will stop and ask: Which species are right for my aquarium community?

Not all the fishes dashing and darting about the tanks before you are suitable for the community aquarium. They may have different preferences when it comes to water chemistry parameters. Some are very placid and may fall prey to the more pugnacious or predatory species that also regularly inhabit the tanks of the average

TROPICAL SPECIES PROFILER:
7 QUESTIONS TO ASK BEFORE BUYING A FISH

1. **How large does it get?** When it reaches adulthood, will it fit into the tank you intend to set up?

2. **How aggressive is it?** What sort of tankmates might it harm?

3. **What does it eat?** Does it have specific dietary requirements that will be difficult to meet or does it have a generalized diet?

4. **Is it piscivorous** (a fish eater) or will it graze on the prize plants you want to keep or devour your prize shrimps or snails?

5. **What are its habitat preferences?** Is it a fish that demands lots of space? Does it have any special aquascaping requirements?

6. **Is it susceptible to disease?**

7. **Is it considered easy or difficult to keep?** Do you have the skills (and resources) to be sure it has a chance to thrive?

pet store. Of course, the members of the latter guild will need to be housed on their own or with other rough and tumble characters.

It is essential to know that many freshwater species offered for sale also attain some amazing sizes. Isn't fish growth suppressed if they are housed in a smaller tank? Just ask anyone who has purchased a juvenile *Phractocephalus hemioliopterus* (a.k.a. the Redtail Catfish) if the growth of these fish is constrained by the size of the tank they are kept in? (Is a St. Bernard puppy brought home to a tiny apartment going to stay small and cute?) The Redtail Catfish can outgrow a smaller tank in no time, and has the capacity to turn into a 4-foot beast.

Most species available to hobbyists do not reach such gargantuan proportions, but it is still important to consider the maximum size of a fish species before you plunk it into your 20-gallon tank.

A lush planted aquarium stocked with a school of Congo Tetras (Phenacogrammus interruptus) and other peaceful species occupying different niches in the tank.

PIRANHAS ON THE LOOSE

Anyone who has worked at a tropical fish shop has seen the results of aquarists making bad choices. In the Midwest, there are numerous stories of startled fisherman pulling large, piranha-like fish out of local lakes. More often than not they are Pacu—big characins belonging to several different genera—not piranhas. These piscine trespassers are usually freed in these lochs because they have outgrown their aquarium homes. Not only does this lead to eventual death for the overgrown tropical (the cold winter will kill it), when exotic introductions are carried out in warmer climes it can lead to ecological disaster. A non-resident fish can have a very deleterious impact on native species, disrupting ancient biological balances and even threatening the very survival of indigenous fishes. Florida and other southern states have many horror stories of aquarium fishes released into local ponds and streams. Major initiatives are underway to discourage hobbyists from dumping their problem fish into wild waterways.

Rash purchases of certain species can also wreak havoc in the home aquarium. I have had friends ask me to visit their tanks to see why they were not having any success, only to find, for example, what was analogous to a 24-hour "cage match" between a colorful Zebra Cichlid (a well known antagonist) and various South American river-dwelling fishes that were cowering in the corners of the tank trying to avoid the domineering bully. Once the territorial African cichlid was removed and returned to the local fish store, things settled down and the mortality rate of the fish in the tank plummeted. It is truly amazing how much unhappiness, loss of fish lives and expense is incurred by hobbyists making naive or reckless choices when they bring home new fishes.

One of the best ways to avoid these problems is to know something about the charges you are going to keep. Knowing some of the biology and natural history of each species not only makes watching them more interesting (you'll understand the unusual behaviors they may exhibit), it will also help you place fish together that will get along and share similar environmental requirements. The aim of this book is to help you make wise choices so you will greatly increase your chances of success rather than having to learn the hard way and at the expense of unfortunate fishes.

THE LAYERING EFFECT

When selecting fish that will make up your aquarium community, you will want to choose species that occupy different microhabitats in the aquarium. If you have ever engaged in landscape design, you know all about microhabitats and creating the layered look. You have your ground cover and shorter plants along the bed borders, your medium-height varieties in the middle of the bed,

*Undeniably cute, a young Oscar (*Astronotus ocellatus*) can easily outgrow the average home aquarium. Some end up illegally released into local waters.*

and your taller forms near the back of the landscape. It looks more interesting and prevents your plants from crowding each other out. We need to utilize a similar methodology when selecting fish species. While fish are not sedentary like plants, there are many that will occupy various "layers" of the aquarium's water column. There are benthic species (bottom-dwelling) that hang near or live on the gravel bed. There are species that tend to hover or swim about in the mid-levels of the aquarium and there are species that tend to stay near the water surface. There are also some species that roam the whole. To make your aquarium more interesting, and to provide more living space for your fishes, you will want species that hang-out in all three layers of the water column. Obviously, these differences in microhabitat use will be more pronounced in a deeper tank.

DITHERFISH & SCHOOLERS

In aquarium circles, ditherers are important and well liked. Dither fishes are active species that are bold and spend most of their time darting about in the open. Their presence serves to have a calming affect on the rest of the fish community. More reclusive or nervous fish species will cue in on the behavior of their neighbors to

Ideal dither fish, a school of White Cloud Mountain Minnows (Tanichthys albonubes) is very effective in giving confidence to shy species and helping to entice them out of hiding and into becoming more competitive at feeding time.

determine if it is safe to come out of hiding. If these fish are not kept with dither species, they are likely to spend more time under cover and less time where the aquarist can observe and enjoy them. Some good dither species include danios and rainbowfishes.

There are also some species that naturally school and will do poorly if kept on their own. These species require the presence of conspecifics to feel secure. Most of these fishes school because there is safety in numbers. Therefore, when they are on their own or in groups that are too small (just two or three when they are accustomed to many more), they sense that they are vulnerable and as a result they are edgy, they feed poorly and are often less colorful. There are tetras, danios, and rainbowfishes that fall into this group. A single Neon Tetra is a lonely and, most likely, very uncomfortable fish.

DEALING WITH AGGRESSION

Aggressive fishes can cause real problems in the confines of the aquarium. Aggression causes stress that can make your fishes more susceptible to disease, even if it doesn't kill a fish outright. An accosted fish may behave abnormally, hanging around in the upper corners of the tank or hiding incessantly. It may eat less and end up starving. It may also exhibit subdued coloration. It is up to us as fish-keepers to populate our tropical fish communities carefully in order to avoid aggression issues. However, there are times when the best-laid plans can be fouled up by a fish that turns into a bad actor.

There are several techniques to help limit the likelihood of aggressive encounters between your fish charges. First of all, and this bears repeating, do not put known belligerent species with those that are timid or peaceful by nature. Always consider a fish's propensity for aggression before turning it loose in your community tank.

Of course, many aquarists are attracted to big, rambunctious or even highly predatory species. If you do have a hankering to house a hellion, be sure its tankmates are like-minded. (The color tags on the edges of each species page will help you delineate between fish of various sizes and dispositions.)

To make things interesting, however, there are numerous species that are not always pugnacious but can become combative or territorial in the confines of a small aquarium. There are also species that fall on or near the line between being peace-loving and moderately aggressive. With these there are a variety of things that might contribute to how they behave in the confines of a home aquarium. These factors include the size of the tank, the density of fish in the community, the order of their introduction to the aquarium, the abundance of hiding places and the physical/behavioral characteristics of their tankmates.

Aquarium size does matter when it comes to aggression. You will have fewer problems with antagonism in a larger tank. Even if you are keeping known bullies, in a large tank there is often enough room for other fishes to avoid them. If the tank is deep, it is likely that substrate-bound species, which tend to be more bellicose, may rarely encounter those fish that live near the water's surface.

With some fishes, you will have better luck if you stock them at higher densities. This, for example, is true with African cichlids. These fish typically form dominance hierarchies in the aquarium. If you have a few in the tank, the individuals at the bottom of the pecking order with be bullied, sometimes to death, by those higher up on the social ladder. However, if you place enough individuals in the tank, a defined hierarchy is more difficult to maintain. Instead of one or two individuals being constantly pestered, aggression is often more evenly distributed throughout the population, with no one fish getting bullied to death.

When putting together your fish wish list, be sure to rank the species according to their propensity to be aggressive, with the most passive species at the top and the most belligerent species at the bottom. This is how you should introduce them to the aquarium— least aggressive first, most aggressive last. This works because prior residence will often impact who is the boss.

If a potential troublemaker is added to the tank first, it is more likely to lay claim to a territory and defend it fiercely against any newcomers. On the other hand, if you start populating the tank with the least territorial fish, there is less likelihood that a moderately aggressive species will later challenge fish that already consider the tank their home. Of course, the always-aggressive species should never be housed with the peaceful types, unless the aquarium is very large. For example, you could have some of the moderately aggressive cichlids in a tank with larger tetras, if the tank is, say, in the 125-gallon (474 L) range and has plenty of places for fishes wanting to seek shelter.

THE HABITAT FACTOR

This brings us to the third factor impacting behavior: aquascaping or tank interior decor. If an aquarium lacks hiding places, then there is more likelihood that the few places available will be defended vigorously by site-attached fish species such as cichlids. However, if there are plenty of hiding places to go around, these squabbles will be less frequent. Also, if a tank is packed with live plants, some of the more passive mid- and upper-water swimmers can seek shelter among the foliage if they feel threatened. Not only does this help prevent their being picked on, it also provides a sense of security that reduces stress levels and allows fish to look their best.

Finally, those fishes that defend a territory tend not to be indiscriminate about who they chase or nip. In the wild, this could be costly to the attacking fish as aggression takes them away from more important activities, such as eating and reproduction, and can

A tankful of South American cichlids with appropriate aquascaping: plenty of rocky shelter, driftwood and plants located where they cannot be uprooted.

make them more prone to being picked off by a lurking predator. Therefore, they tend to go after those species that compete with them for resources, like food, shelter and mates.

PROFILING YOUR FISHES

For the reasons stated, a territorial fish is going to be most aggressive toward conspecifics (they have the most resource overlap). Next on the list are usually those species that have similar food habits. For example, an algae-grazing cichlid is most likely to assault another fish that shares its dietary proclivities. But how do they know which fish are food competitors? Typically, fish that feed on the same foods are similar in form and behavior. Therefore, a territorial fish will usually attack another fish that looks like it (form and/or color) and one that behaves like it. There are some other ways to reduce the likelihood of aggression when you are adding a new fish to the tank. Some of these techniques can be especially useful when

A pair of Betta splendens, *the Siamese Fighting Fish, with female at left: a species with a rich history and a repertoire of interesting behaviors when given swimming room, correct water temperature, and appropriate tankmates.*

placing moderately aggressive or highly aggressive fishes together in the same tank.

Finally, I like to use the analogy of buying a new puppy. The happiest dog owners are the ones who spent some time researching the differences between breeds before making their final choice. Tropical fishkeepers who make the effort to ask questions about fishes that catch their eye and who make the effort to look up the profile of a new species are invariably happier with their aquariums.

It is also worth knowing that, with reasonable care, certain tropical fishes can live more than 10 years, and 20 years is not unheard of. Choose the right fish and it has the potential to become a pet for years to come. Using this and other guidebooks, tapping the experiences of other aquarists and informed store staff members can go a long way to helping you evade the predictable headaches and heartbreaks that result when we put the wrong species together in the microcosmic world of a home aquarium.

CURBING AGGRESSION: TRICKS & TACTICS

Several approaches and tricks can be followed to help control aggression toward incoming specimens:

- **Add the least-aggressive fish species first** and the most belligerent last.

- **Do not overcrowd** your aquarium. More space per fish equals less aggression. That said, in some cases, crowding certain fish species, such as African cichlids, can reduce the likelihood that any one fish is harassed to death.

- **Provide plenty of functional hiding places.**

- **Break up aquarium aquascaping** into numerous smaller rocky mounds rather than one larger one if you have a larger tank.

- **Avoid keeping conspecifics or closely related species** in the same tank, especially if the tank is small.

- **Avoid keeping similarly shaped or colored species,** particularly if one of them is known to be aggressive.

- **Turn off the lights** when introducing a new fish.

- **Feed resident fish first** before adding a new fish.

- **Rearrange aquascaping** before adding new fish.

- **Place the fish in a clear container**, like a plastic gallon jar with holes in it, or partition off a portion of the tank with a clear piece of acrylic, and let the residents grow accustomed to the new introduction for a several days or more before removing it from the enclosure.

- **Add a small mirror to the aquarium** to divert some of the resident fishes' aggression.

- **Isolate the aggressor for several days** in a quarantine tank and then reintroduce it when the new fish is established.

A tranquil community tank by master aquarist Takashi Amano shows the magic that can happen with the right combination of fishes, plants and aquascaping.

Inspiration for mixing and matching tropical fishes

The curious reality is that most people give more thought to what they toss into their salad bowls than the fishes they add to their first community aquariums. The traditional community-style tank contains a wide variety of species, many—if not most—of which will never meet in nature. There is nothing wrong with this, and one of the great things about tropical fishkeeping is being free to populate our tanks as we see fit. Still, we are dealing with living creatures and there are limits to what we can put together in the same box of water. There are two main things to keep in mind when assembling a new community: 1. Picking fishes that will be able to live happily in the same environmental conditions (light, temperature, water chemistry, aquascaping, feeding). 2. Not picking fishes that will eat their tankmates or bully them until they starve or are harassed to death.

Use this guide to find and know more about the species that get your attention. With their different sizes and requirements in mind, create a plan for your own underwater world. To start the thought process and to highlight some combinations that expert aquarists have found to work, here are some model communities that can easily be replicated using species found in this guide. For the typical neophyte ready to start with a 10-gallon tank, we offer some nicely balanced starter communities.

10-Gallon (38 L) Peaceful Global Community

Here is a winning combination of colorful, hardy, peaceful species that provide top to bottom action and interest.

Top Swimmers
2 Dwarf Gouramis (Male-Female pair)   *Colisa lalia*

Midwater Swimmers
5-7 Glowlight Tetras   *Hemigrammus erythrozonus*

Bottom Dwellers
3 Albino Aeneus Corydoras Catfish   *Corydoras aeneus*
2 Otocinclus Catfish   *Otocinclus vittatus*

Panda Corydoras scavenge uneaten food and are small enough for any tank.

AQUARIUM CARRYING CAPACITY

There are a number of factors that will determine the carrying capacity of your aquarium. If you overcrowd your tank, water quality will deteriorate rapidly (e.g., declining pH, nitrate buildup, low oxygen levels). There is also a greater likelihood of behavioral problems, namely aggression. Poor water quality and antagonism increase fish stress levels which make your aquarium charges more susceptible to disease, listlessness, color loss and other ailments. Therefore, it is always better to have one or two fish too few, than one or two fish too many!

It is hard to know exactly how many fish an aquarium can sustain. The most common rule of thumb for a well-maintained, properly set-up, tropical fish aquarium is one inch of fish per gallon of tank. (These inch-per-gallon equations have inherent problems, but are "aquarist-friendly" and typically give us a good starting point.) It is very important to reach the carrying capacity very slowly. You should add approximately 20% of the tank's carrying capacity in fish in the first week. For example, if you have a 20-gallon tank, add 4 inches of fish. Wait several more weeks before adding more fish—then you can add another 20% of the tank's carrying capacity (that, of course, would be another 4 inches in our 20-gallon aquarium). Continue to do this every couple of weeks until you reach about 80 to 90% of the carrying capacity (in our 20-gallon tank that would be 16 to 18 inches of fish). With luck, the extra 10 to 20% will cover future growth.

10-Gallon (38 L) Amazon Quiet Pool

Bringing together species from the same geographic region is called a biotope approach and it can make for some of the most interesting and authentic communities.

Top Swimmers
| 3 Marbled Hatchetfish | *Carnegiella strigata* |

Midwater Swimmers
| 12 Neon Tetras | *Paracheirodon innesi* |

Bottom Dwellers
| 3 Panda Corydoras | *Corydoras panda* |
| 1 Clown Pleco | *Panaque maccus* |

10-Gallon (38 L) Malaysian Slow Stream

Here is an Asian biotope with great, compatible species and something happening from the upper layer to bottom where the loaches will play.

Top Swimmers
| 5 Glass Catfish | *Kryptopterus minor* |
—or
| 5 Harlequin Rasbora | *Trigonostigma heteromorpha* |

Midwater Swimmers
| 3 Cherry Barbs | *Puntius titteya* |

Bottom Dwellers
| 3 Kuhli Loach | *Pangio kuhlii* |
| 3 Dwarf Loach | *Yasuhikotakia sidthimunki* |

10-Gallon (38 L) Dwarf-Cichlid Nesting Tank

Here's a tank designed with mild-mannered tankmates and pair of beautiful dwarf cichlids that are likely to spawn. This same community would also fit nicely into a 15- or 20-gallon aquarium with the addition of more peaceful midwater swimming tetras and two additional female cichlids to form a harem.

Midwater to Top Swimmers
| 4 Lemon Tetras | *Hyphessobrycon pulchripinnis* |

Bottom Dwellers
| 2 Cockatoo Dwarf Cichlids (pair) | *Apistogramma cacatuoides* |
| 3 Threestripe Corydoras Catfish | *Corydoras trilineatus* |

10-Gallon (38 L) Livebearer Community

This community offers flash, color galore and the prospect of frequent birthing events. Dense plantings will give the newborn fry places to hide. A second rearing tank for the babies would be a good addition.

Midwater to Top Swimmers
6 Fancy Guppies (2 males : 4 females)   *Poecilia reticulata*
3 Swordtails (1 male : 2 females)   *Xiphophorus helleri*

Bottom
3 Bronze Corydoras   *Corydoras aeneus*

20-Gallon (76 L) Amazon Backwater Community

Here is a winning combination of South American species sure to provide long hours of viewing pleasure. Choose a "long" tank to accommodate the active surface-cruising hatchetfish.

Top Swimmers
2 Silver Hatchetfish   *Gasteropelecus sternicla*

Midwater Swimmers
1 Trio Emperor Tetras (1 male : 2 females) *Nematobrycon palmeri*
5 Lemon Tetras   *Hyphessobrycon pulchripinnis*

Bottom Dwellers
3 Peppered Corydoras Catfish   *Corydoras paleatus*

Cardinal Tetras and their characin kin will put on a constant show of natural behaviors when kept in schools of at least four and up to 50 or more fish.

20-Gallon (Long) Peaceful Asian Community

Asia offers a wealth of choices for anyone assembling a community of beautiful but mild-mannered fishes. This tank has a Zen-like calm when well planted and given some natural driftwood.

Top Swimmers
| 3-6 Glass Catfish | *Kryptopterus minor* |

Midwater Swimmers
| 3-6 Harlequin Rasbora | *Trigonostigma heteromorpha* |

Bottom Dwellers
3 Dwarf Loaches	*Yasuhikotakia sidthimunki*
3 Kuhli Loaches	*Pangio kuhlii*
1 Siamese Algae Eater	*Crossocheilus siamensis*

20-Gallon South American Quiet Ram Community

This tank sets up a peaceful breeding environment for a pair of dwarf cichlids with dither fish and no threatening species.

Midwater Swimmers
| 6 Cardinal Tetras | *Paracheirodon axelrodi* |
| —or 6 Neon Tetras | *Paracheirodon innesi* |

Bottom Dwellers
2 Ram Dwarf Cichlids (pair)	*Microgeophagus ramirezi*
6 Pygmy Cory Catfish	*Corydoras pygmaeus*
1 Bushynose Pleco	*Ancistrus spp.*

30-Gallon Asian Delightful Community

The big, colorful gouramis are the centerpiece of this tank and will very likely put on displays of classic bubblenest building and spawning.

Top Swimmers
| 2 Pearl Gouramis (pair) | *Trichogaster leerii* |
| —or 2 Blue Gouramis (pair) | *Trichogaster trichopterus* |

Midwater Swimmers.
4-6 Checkerboard Barbs	*Puntius oligolepis*
—or	
8-10 Harlequin Rasbora	*Trigonostigma heteromorpha*

Bottom Dwellers
| 4 Dwarf Loach | *Yasuhikotakia sidthimunki* |

30-Gallon—Asian Active Community

Here is a tankful of movement and fishes that can take care of themselves but that are not overly aggressive. The Botia may eventually outgrow this system, so plan accordingly.

Midwater Swimmers
4-6 Black Ruby Barbs   *Puntius nigrofasciatus*
—or
4-6 Rosy Barbs   *Puntius conchonius*
Bottom Dwellers
2 Siamese Algae Eaters   *Crossocheilus siamensis*
3 Redtail Botia   *Yasuhikotakia modesta*

30-Gallon Upside-Down Catfish African Community

This unusual tank highlights the schooling behaviors of the little Upside-down Catfish with its inverted underwater swimming ballet. The peaceful tetras add color and act as dither fish, giving the cichlids a sense of confidence about their environment.

Top Swimmers
6 Upside-down Catfish   *Synodontis nigriventris*
Midwater Swimmers
3-5 Redeye Tetras   *Arnoldichthys spilopterus*
Bottom Dwellers
2 Ram Dwarf Cichlids (pair)   *Microgeophagus ramirezi*

30-Gallon Convict Community

The Convict Cichlids are the focal point, but the supporting cast adds much interest and color to all levels of the aquascape.

Top Swimmers
6-7 Non-fancy Guppies   *Poecilia reticulata*
—or
3 Swordtails (1 male : 2 females)   *Xiphophorus helleri*
Midwater Swimmers
4-6 Bleeding Heart Tetras   *Hyphessobrycon erythrostigma*
Bottom Dwellers
2-3 Convict Cichlids   *Amatitlania nigrofasciatus*
3-4 Emerald Catfish   *Brochis splendens*

30-Gallon Lake Malawi Mixed Community

The Rainbowfish are not native to Lake Malawi but are useful in communities with African cichlids to act as dither fish that move constantly and help dispel hostile confrontations within species.

Top to Midwater Swimmers
3-4 Rainbowfishes	*Melanotaenia* sp.

Bottom Dwellers
3 Yellow Labidos	*Labidochromis caeruleus*
2-3 Cuckoo Catfish	*Synodontis multipunctatus*
3-4 Emerald Catfish	*Brochis splendens*

50-Gallon African Tank

Take the time and let the Congo Tetras grow to full maturity and you will experience a tank of true beauty. The lovely African Butterfly Cichlids will likely spawn with proper feeding and good water.

Midwater Swimmers
8-12 Congo Tetras	*Phenacogrammus interruptus*

Bottom Dwellers
2 African Butterfly Cichlids (pair)	*Anomalochromis thomasi*
2-3 Marbled Synodontis Catfish	*Synodontis schoutedeni*

Rainbowfishes such as this Boeseman's Rainbow can serve as dither species in tanks of large cichlids, adding constant movement to distract aggression.

35

50-Gallon Mouthbrooder Breeding Tank

This community is planned as a display for a pair of mouthbrooders, either Finley's Cichlid in which both parents play a role or Gunther's Cichlid with the male being the initial caretaker.

3-4 Finley's Cichlid	*Benitochromis finleyi*
–or	
3-4 Gunther's Mouthbrooder	*Chromidotilapia guntheri*
5-7 Congo Tetras	*Phenacogrammus interruptus*
2-3 Upside-down Catfish	*Synodontis nigriventris*

50-Gallon Oscar Species Tank

Here is an odd-couple tank that allows the keeper to cultivate a "pet" Oscar along with a big, self-sufficient catfish that can hold its own in the presence of a large cichlid.

1 Oscar	*Astronotus ocellatus*
1 Leopard Pleco	*Pterygoplichthys gibbiceps*
–or	
1 Spotted or Striped Raphael	*Platydoras sp.*

50-Gallon South American Angelfish Community

With thickets of Amazon Swordplants of various sizes, this community sets the stage for a group of small angelfish to mature into a breeding pair that will end up reigning over their watery kingdom.

Top Swimmers

3-4 Marbled Hatchetfish	*Carnegiella strigata*

Midwater Swimmers

3-6 Angelfish	*Pterophyllum scalare*
4-6 Black Phantom Tetras	*Megalamphodus megalopterus*
4-6 Rummynose Tetras	*Hemigrammus sp.*
–or	
4-6 Diamond Tetras	*Moenkhausia pittieri*

Bottom Dwellers

1 Hoplo Catfish	*Megalechis thoracata*
1-2 Bushynose Plecos	*Ancistrus sp.*

Angelfishes become majestic as they mature but require tankmates that are neither too small nor likely to interfere with their spawning behaviors.

Tiger Barbs are ever-popular and
a hardy choice for the right community tank.

A field guide to aquarium fishes: species that can thrive for you

For the tropical fish enthusiast, bringing home a new fish—one whose native habitat might be a Rift Lake in Africa, a rice paddy in Mayalasia, a remote stream in Papua New Guinea or a jungle pool in the upper reaches of the Amazon basin is one of life's pulse-quickening moments.

To know that you are not bringing home a bag full of trouble or a fish that has little chance of surviving in your particular home aquarium, the following 101 species are presented as great choices, especially for less-experienced freshwater aquarists—or those who want to improve the odds that their new acquistions will thrive.

For simplicity, the species are arranged in alphabetical order by common name of the family or group—Barbs, Catfishes, Danios and so on, and then by common name of each species.

COLOR KEY TO SIZES

One of the most important criteria for selection of a fish is its eventual adult size. Will it fit in your aquarium? Will it be an appropriate tankmate for your other fishes or fishes you plan to buy? The cute baby Oscar that can grow into a foot-long, greedy predator that eats all your fancy guppies may not be the best choice.

Here is the Size Key used in this guide:

SMALL (or NANO):
Requires minimum aquarium size of 10-30 gal. (38-114 L)

MEDIUM:
Requires minimum aquarium size of 50-75 gal. (190-285 L)

LARGE:
Requires minimum aquarium size of 100-180 gal. (380-684 L)

STOCKING SLOWLY

One word of caution: when buying new fish, don't acquire too many at any one time. It is often tempting to load up on livestock when you drive some distance to buy fish or order from a mail-order fish supplier. Some impulsive fish shoppers can't handle having so many choices at their fingertips and end up with more fish than they can safely introduce at one time. The problem is that quarantine space (see pages 171-173) is often limited. This means you'll end up crowding fish in your quarantine tank or, even worse, introducing them directly into the display tank because of space limitations. Either situation all too often ends in disaster. You will be better able to monitor and treat one or two individuals (or a school of a single species) at a time in your quarantine tank, rather than five or six different fish.

Finally, buying aquarium fishes sight-unseen is a questionable practice, unless you use a known, reputable supplier. Most experienced aquarists much prefer to see what they are getting in a local shop and, perhaps, paying a little more. *"Think Global, Buy Local"* is not a bad rule in today's wired world, and it holds especially true in buying live aquarium fish.

LOOKING BEFORE LEAPING

Take your time in selecting a new fish from a dealer's tanks. See a fish you particularly like? Here's a quick checklist of things to ask and watch for before making the decision to buy it.

3 QUESTIONS: A FISH-BUYER'S CHECKLIST
Things to ask before bringing home a new fish:

1. **Is the specimen** you are considering alert, clear of wounds or signs of disease (white spots, patches of unhealthy skin or ragged fins).

2. **Is this fish eating?** (If in doubt, ask them to feed the fish and be sure that it has a healthy interest in food.)

3. **How long** has the dealer had the fish? (If it has just arrived, you may want to have them hold it for a few days or a week to be sure it recovers from the stresses of shipping.)

BETTA *Betta splendens*
(Siamese Fighting Fish)

MAXIMUM LENGTH: 2.3 in. (6 cm).
NATIVE RANGE: Thailand, Cambodia.
MINIMUM AQUARIUM SIZE: 2 gal. (7.6 L).
GENERAL SWIMMING LEVEL: Every level of the tank.
OVERVIEW: The glorious finnage and fight-to-the-death spirit of male bettas can be traced back almost 175 years to breeders in Thailand (then Siam). Males are usually kept singly, but Bettas can be fine community fish if kept with no aggressive or fin-nipping species. One male to two females is best, as the male can be pretty rough at times, and the presence of two females will dilute his aggression.
FEEDING: Omnivore. Feed a variety of meaty, high-protein foods supplemented with color-enhancing flake foods.
HABITAT: A well-planted tank with dark substrate will reveal this lovely fish as a true "show-off" with a surprising amount of personality. Bettas are from the tropics and require constant warm temperatures in the range of 78-80°F (26-27°C). Floating plants will be used for hiding and nest building.
AQUARIUM CARE/BEHAVIOR: Like all labyrinthfishes, the Betta has an auxiliary breathing apparatus (labyrinth) that allows it to breathe air at the water's surface and survive in small tanks or containers.
BREEDING: When the male builds his floating nest of saliva-coated air bubbles, he is ready to breed. A pair will "embrace" in open water, releasing both eggs and sperm. The male gathers the fertilized eggs after each embrace and spits them up into the bubblenest. The male tends the eggs, which hatch after 24 hours.

BLACK RUBY BARB *Puntius nigrofasciatus*
(Purple-headed or Ruby-headed Barb)

MAXIMUM LENGTH: 2.3 in. (6 cm).

NATIVE RANGE: Sri Lanka.

MINIMUM AQUARIUM SIZE: 20-29 gal. (76-110 L), long.

GENERAL SWIMMING LEVEL: Midwater.

OVERVIEW: A school of barbs with their prominent, light-reflective scales, brings flash and color to any community aquarium. The short whiskers or barbels near the mouth are used for finding food in the substrate and give these fish their common name. During spawning, males develop a bright crimson-red body and a red tail fin.

FEEDING: Omnivore. Barbs are easy to feed and will accept a wide variety of meaty aquarium fare, as well as frozen and live foods and herbivore foods.

HABITAT: As with most Cyprinids (minnow-type fishes), habitat for the Black Ruby Barb is more about providing sufficient open areas for swimming than actual decor. They are best kept in a long, rather than tall, aquarium, with plants restricted to the sides and back or a layer of floating plants at the surface. Decorate sparingly with driftwood and provide a dark fine-grade gravel substrate to help show off their bright colors.

AQUARIUM CARE/BEHAVIOR: Like other barbs, this is an active schooling species best kept in groups of at least three, with a variety of community tank residents like other barbs and danios. Susceptible to poor water quality, so regular water changes are a must.

BREEDING: Egg scatterers that spawn adhesive eggs among plants and will greedily eat their own eggs.

CHECKERBOARD *Barb Puntius oligolepis*
(Checker or Checkered Barb, Island Barb)

MAXIMUM LENGTH: 2 in. (5 cm)

NATIVE RANGE: Sumatra, Indonesia.

MINIMUM AQUARIUM SIZE: 20 gal. (76 L), long.

GENERAL SWIMMING LEVEL: Midwater.

OVERVIEW: This is a distinctive, peaceful schooling species once known as the Island Barb as it was found only on the big island of Sumatra. Mature males have red fins with black tips. This species sports a small pair of barbels.

FEEDING: Omnivore. *Puntius oligolepis* feeds on worms, small crustaceans, insects and plant matter in the wild and will accept all types of fairly fine-grade foods, such as flakes, freeze-dried and frozen varieties. Include vegetable-based foods like *Spirulina* wafers or flakes.

HABITAT: As with most of its family, the primary focus of a tank for Checkerboard Barbs should be lots of room to swim. Keep plants and other decor to a minimum, mostly on the sides and back of the aquarium, leaving plenty of open space in the center for swimming. Long tanks are best.

AQUARIUM CARE/BEHAVIOR: It is best kept in groups of at least three. Males may display toward one another, but this is mainly for show and rarely results in injury. The Checkerboard Barb is an active schooling species that does well in most community tank settings, as long as there is plenty of room to swim.

BREEDING: These are typical egg scatterers that shed adhesive eggs among bushy plants and will eat their own spawn if the eggs and adults are not separated.

CHERRY BARB *Puntius titteya*

MAXIMUM LENGTH: 2 in. (5 cm).

NATIVE RANGE: Sri Lanka.

MINIMUM AQUARIUM SIZE: 20 gal. (76 L), long.

GENERAL SWIMMING LEVEL: Midwater.

OVERVIEW: A classic aquarium species, this small, slender Barb is torpedo-shaped with chameleon-like color variations in different conditions and different strains. The female is often light, iridescent pink, while the male is darker. The anal and tail fins of the male are bright cherry red. An albino morph is now being propagated.

FEEDING: Omnivore. In the wild, the Cherry Barb feeds mostly on vegetable matter, but will accept a wide variety of prepared aquarium fare, including good-quality flakes. Their diets must include algae and plant matter, including *Spirulina*-based foods. Treat occasionally with frozen or live brine shrimp or bloodworms.

HABITAT: Provide lots of open swimming room with plantings kept mostly at the back and ends of the tank, and a cover of floating plants. Barbs need a fine-grade or rounded gravel substrate to burrow in. Will nibble on plants and perform light algae cleanup.

AQUARIUM CARE/BEHAVIOR: The Cherry Barb is a timid, schooling species that should be kept in groups of at least four with smaller community tank residents. Regular water changes are a plus.

BREEDING: Extremely easy to breed, Cherry Barbs scatter their adhesive eggs among plants, and should be immediately removed or they will eat the eggs. May jump out of the aquarium when spawning, so a tight-fitting cover is a must.

GOLD BARB *Puntius semifasciolatus*
(Shubert's Barb, Green Barb, Half-Striped Barb, Chinese Barb)

MAXIMUM LENGTH: 3 in. (7 cm).
NATIVE RANGE: Southeastern China.
MINIMUM AQUARIUM SIZE: 20 gal. (76 L).
GENERAL SWIMMING LEVEL: Midwater.

OVERVIEW: The Gold Barb is an active, out-going fish. Decades of selective breeding have transformed the rather plain wild fish into glittering aquarium beauties. The Gold Barb is unusual among freshwater fishes in showing some green coloration. Males tend to be smaller and more intensely colored.

FEEDING: Omnivore. The Gold Barb is a hearty eater that will accept just about any aquarium fare, including flake and freeze-dried foods. Some vegetable matter is a must, so include *Spirulina*-based foods as well. Occasional treats of frozen or live foods, including brine shrimp, are also appreciated.

HABITAT: Like most of the other barbs, the Gold Barb does best in a long aquarium, well-planted on the sides and back with plenty of open room in the center for swimming. Because they may root around in the substrate, use only fine-grade or rounded gravel.

AQUARIUM CARE/BEHAVIOR: The Gold Barb is a typical Barb—an active schooling species that is best kept in groups of at least three. It is a great fish for a community setting with other peaceful and active species.

BREEDING: This species is known for its readiness to spawn. Adhesive eggs are scattered among plants. Eggs will be eaten if not removed.

BARB – CYPRINID • PEACEFUL

ROSY BARB *Puntius conchonius*

MAXIMUM LENGTH: 5.5 in. (14 cm).

NATIVE RANGE: India.

MINIMUM AQUARIUM SIZE: 20 gal. (76 L).

GENERAL SWIMMING LEVEL: Midwater.

OVERVIEW: Here is a legendarily hardy fish, ideal for beginners. It is durable, easy to feed and brings nice action to any tank when kept in a school. During spawning, the male becomes deep red. Long-finned varieties have been developed and are often available.

FEEDING: Omnivore. The Rosy Barb will accept most commercial meaty and vegetable-based aquarium fare, including good-quality *Spirulina* flakes, algae wafers and color-enhancing rations.

HABITAT: The Rosy Barb is one of the more durable barbs and is tolerant of cooler water temperatures. As with most of the Barbs, decor is strictly for the aquarist, as are plants, which can be restricted to the sides and back of the tank. They need lots of open swimming space, which is easier to provide in a longer, rather than tall, aquarium. Because the Rosy Barb may root around in the gravel, a fine-grade substrate is best. Darker colors (substrate and background) well help show off the fish's colors and make them feel more secure.

AQUARIUM CARE/BEHAVIOR: The Rosy Barb is not quite as rambunctious as the Tiger Barb. This is a schooling species that should be kept in groups of at least three. Rowdy cichlids or lone tiger barbs may harass them.

BREEDING: Great species for beginning breeders. If well fed and kept with clumps of bushy plants, spawning events are almost inevitable.

TIGER BARB *Puntius tetrazona*
(Sumatra Barb)

MAXIMUM LENGTH: 2.75 in. (7 cm).

NATIVE RANGE: Sumatra and Borneo.

MINIMUM AQUARIUM SIZE: 30 gal. (114 L).

GENERAL SWIMMING LEVEL: Midwater.

OVERVIEW: The Tiger Barb is a wonderful little fish with distinctive stripes and a spirited personality. A large school makes an impressive display. The Tiger Barb today is mostly commercially bred and comes in a variety of color morphs, including albino and moss green.

FEEDING: Omnivore. Tiger Barbs are good eaters that will accept any aquarium fare they can fit in their mouths, including flakes and pellets. Supplement their diets with frozen and live foods, such as brine shrimp and black worms, and include vegetable matter like *Spirulina*-based foods.

HABITAT: It makes little difference if the plants are live or plastic, as the Tiger Barb is not known to be tough on greenery. What is important is to leave plenty of open areas for swimming.

AQUARIUM CARE/BEHAVIOR: The Tiger Barb is an active schooling species that should be kept in groups of at least three to avoid becoming a fin-nipping nuisance. Keep with fishes of similar size and temperament and avoid long-finned tankmates, such as angelfish and bettas.

BREEDING: Adult Tiger Barbs will spawn in a community aquarium, although it is unlikely that any of the eggs will escape being eaten. If you wish to raise the fry, use a separate breeding tank with clumps of *Cabomba* or other bushy plants.

ASIAN BUMBLEBEE CATFISH *Pseudomystus siamensis*

MAXIMUM LENGTH: 6 in. (15 cm).

NATIVE RANGE: Southeast Asia.

MINIMUM AQUARIUM SIZE: 30 gal. (114 L).

GENERAL SWIMMING LEVEL: Bottom.

OVERVIEW: The Asian Bumblebee Catfish is a fascinating addition to collections of larger fishes and a favorite among catfish enthusiasts. It may make an audible noise when removed from the water. It will do best in a community of species that can fend for themselves as this catfish may nip fins and eat small fishes.

FEEDING: Carnivore. This species consumes insects and small aquatic crustaceans in the wild, but will adapt to most commercial meaty catfish foods in the aquarium, including good-quality flakes, pellets, sinking wafers with shrimp, as well as live and frozen foods, such as bloodworms, *Tubifex* worms and brine shrimp. Feed first thing in the morning and just after the lights go out at night.

HABITAT: The Asian Bumblebee Catfish needs a tank with sufficient caves in the form of stones, inverted flowerpots, large black PVC pipe, or rock piles with openings throughout, to provide each fish its own cave. Decorate with driftwood and artificial or live plants.

AQUARIUM CARE/BEHAVIOR: *Pseudomystus siamensis* may be territorial and aggressive. Continuous clicking noises during the night may signal potential aggressive interactions, and it may be necessary to remove the belligerent culprits. Do not keep with fishes small enough to fit into their mouths.

BREEDING: Not reported in the aquarium, but may lay its eggs among roots in the wild.

BRONZE CORYDORAS *Corydoras aeneus*
(Green Corydoras, Aeneus Catfish)

MAXIMUM LENGTH: 2.75 in. (7 cm).
NATIVE RANGE: Trinidad and widespread in South America.
MINIMUM AQUARIUM SIZE: 20 gal. (76 L).
GENERAL SWIMMING LEVEL: Bottom.
OVERVIEW: All of the many "Cory" species are delightful, modestly sized catfish that are perfect for a beginner's aquarium. This species is the mainstay of the group. They are all "armored" catfishes with two main rows of overlapping, bony plates on their bodies. The Bronze Corydoras is a schooling species that should be kept in groups of at least three to best observe their natural behaviors.
FEEDING: Omnivore. Considered scavengers, these fishes are often neglected when it comes to feeding. They must be fed in the morning and just after the lights are extinguished at night to ensure optimum health and prepare them for spawning. Will accept a wide variety of meaty and herbivore aquarium fare, including flakes and pellets, especially those specifically designed for corys.
HABITAT: The Bronze Corydoras will be seen continually and industriously searching the substrate for food. The best choice is either fine-grade or rounded gravel. Provide hiding places, such as driftwood, rocks and inverted flowerpots.
AQUARIUM CARE/BEHAVIOR: Their constant grubbing keeps the substrate well stirred and free of stagnant pockets.
BREEDING: The larger female carries fertilized eggs between her ventral fins and deposits them on glass panes, leaves or stones. Fry are easily raised in a well-established tank with a layer of mulm.

ALBINO AENEUS CORYDORAS CATFISH
Corydoras aeneus albino
Length: 2.75 in. (7 cm).

AXELROD'S CORYDORAS CATFISH
Corydoras axelrodi
Length: 2 in. (5 cm).

PANDA CORYDORAS CATFISH
Corydoras panda
Length: 1.75 in. (4.5 cm).

PEPPERED CORYDORAS CATFISH
Corydoras paleatus
Length: 3 in. (7.6 cm).

SKUNK CORYDORAS CATFISH
Corydoras arcuatus
Length: 2.5 in. (6.4 cm).

THREESTRIPE CORYDORAS CATFISH
Corydoras trilineatus
Length: 2.5 in. (6.4 cm).

PYGMY CORY *Corydoras pygmaeus*

MAXIMUM LENGTH: 1 in. (2.5 cm).

NATIVE RANGE: Northern South America.

MINIMUM AQUARIUM SIZE: 10 gal. (38 L).

GENERAL SWIMMING LEVEL: Bottom to midwater.

OVERVIEW: This is the smallest of the corys and a truly delightful fish that makes an ideal resident for a small, peaceful community aquarium. Unlike most other corys, they prefer to swim midwater, and spend most of their time searching every nook and cranny in the aquarium for tidbits of food. They also seem to enjoy chasing one another about the aquarium.

FEEDING: Carnivore. The Pygmy Cory will accept a wide variety of commercial aquarium fare, including finely crushed flakes, crushed pellets and sinking wafers, especially those specifically designed for corys. They will also greedily accept either live, frozen or freeze-dried *Tubifex* worms, brine shrimp, *Daphnia* and bloodworms as an occasional treat. To ensure good health, they must be fed first thing in the morning and just after the lights are extinguished at night.

HABITAT: The Pygmy Cory is best kept in a densely planted aquarium, with a large open area in the center for swimming. Provide plenty of hiding places in the form of driftwood and other aquarium woods, or inverted flowerpots.

AQUARIUM CARE/BEHAVIOR: *Corydoras pygmaeus* should only be kept in groups of three or more—the more you can keep, the better. Tankmates must be very small, very peaceful species.

BREEDING: Males are smaller and more slender than females. Spawns in pairs or groups and attaches adhesive eggs to plants.

DWARF SUCKERMOUTH *Otocinclus vestitus*
(Otocinclus Catfish)

MAXIMUM LENGTH: 1.25 in. (3.3 cm).

NATIVE RANGE: Brazil, Peru, Bolivia.

MINIMUM AQUARIUM SIZE: 10 gal. (38 L).

GENERAL SWIMMING LEVEL: Bottom and on all substrates.

OVERVIEW: Members of the genus *Otocinclus* are busy little fishes and nothing if not thorough when it comes to suctioning leaves and other substrate of green algae. Several similar species, including the Golden Dwarf Suckermouth (*O. affinis*) are often available.

FEEDING: Herbivore. A common mistake is assuming that because the Dwarf Suckermouth eats algae in nature, it can survive with no additional feedings in the aquarium. This is, in fact, not true, and many an *Otocinclus* has paid the price. Feed a varied diet of commercial flake, pelleted and sinking wafers designed for suckermouth catfishes, as well as garden vegetables sunk to the bottom. Feed first thing in the morning and just after the lights go out at night.

HABITAT: Keep in an aquarium with wide-leaved plants, such as *Echinodorus*, with plenty of driftwood on which the catfish can browse as well. Provide a smooth, rounded gravel substrate, as they also search the substrate for food.

AQUARIUM CARE/BEHAVIOR: The Dwarf Suckermouth should be kept in groups of at least three in mostly peaceful, planted community aquarium settings.

BREEDING: Spawn much like Corydoras, on just about any surface—glass, rock, leaf—onto which they can place their adhesive spawn. Afterwards, there is no parental care of the eggs.

EMERALD CATFISH *Brochis splendens*

MAXIMUM LENGTH: 3 in. (7.6 cm).
NATIVE RANGE: Peru, Brazil, Ecuador.
MINIMUM AQUARIUM SIZE: 20 gal. (76 L).
GENERAL SWIMMING LEVEL: Bottom.
OVERVIEW: A peaceful, undemanding fish, ideal for community settings and the beginner's aquarium. Keep in groups of at least three to fully enjoy their wonderful antics. The gorgeous, metallic emerald sheen seen in healthy Emerald Catfishes only develops if good water quality is maintained.
FEEDING: Omnivore. In the wild, these fishes feed on aquatic insect larvae and other foods they find sifting through the substrate. They will accept a wide variety of commercial fare, including flakes and catfish wafers containing shrimp, as well as live and frozen foods, such as brine shrimp, bloodworms and *Tubifex* worms. Feed first thing in the morning and just after the lights go out at night.
HABITAT: Because this species sifts through the gravel and may injure its barbels, a tank for the Emerald Catfish should have a fine-grade or smooth, rounded gravel substrate. Densely plant with live or artificial plants and leave plenty of places for refuge, including inverted flowerpots and driftwood.
AQUARIUM CARE/BEHAVIOR: Avoid substantially larger and aggressive tankmates, such as large cichlids. (This species is sometimes confused with *Corydoras aeneus*, but is somewhat larger and has more rays in the dorsal fin. Compare to photo on page 49.)
BREEDING: Captive spawning is uncommon. Will spawn in groups and lay eggs on plants and tank sides.

GLASS CATFISH *Kryptopterus minor*
(Ghost Catfish, Asian Glass Catfish)

MAXIMUM LENGTH: 2.75 in. (7 cm).

NATIVE RANGE: Indonesia, western Borneo, Thailand.

MINIMUM AQUARIUM SIZE: 20 gal. (76 L).

GENERAL SWIMMING LEVEL: Middle and upper half.

OVERVIEW: The Glass Catfish is virtually transparent and aquarium watchers delight in spotting a ghostly school of them weaving among the plantings extending their long, feeler-like barbels. The silvery pouch of internal organs and the fine skeletal bones are the most telltale signs that these fish are present. This is a graceful, retiring fish that will do best in a well-planted tank with no aggressive tankmates. The Glass or Ghost Catfish is frequently sold as *Kryptopterus bicirrhis*.

FEEDING: Carnivore. The Glass Catfish can be coaxed to accept flake or other floating meaty foods if the foods are placed in the current. They will be best maintained on small- to medium-size live foods, such as *Daphnia*, *Tubifex* worms and glass worms. Feed first thing in the morning and just after the lights go out at night.

HABITAT: The Glass Catfish is rather timid and needs lush clumps of plants to give it a sense of security.

AQUARIUM CARE/BEHAVIOR: This is a schooling species that should be kept in groups of at least four (preferably more) in a community tank with small, peaceful species. Good filtration and a slight amount of water movement is beneficial.

BREEDING: It is known to be an open-water spawner that releases its eggs above plants. No instances reported in the aquarium.

HOPLO *Megalechis thoracata*
(Bubblenest Catfish, Brown Hoplo)

MAXIMUM LENGTH: 6 in. (15 cm).
NATIVE RANGE: Northern South America.
MINIMUM AQUARIUM SIZE: 30 gal. (114 L).
GENERAL SWIMMING LEVEL: Bottom to midwater.
OVERVIEW: The Hoplo is an attractive catfish as a juvenile, with a speckled body pattern on a brown background. It is a mainstay among catfish fanciers, but it becomes less attractive with age as the colors may soften. The Hoplo is relatively peaceful but somewhat disruptive in quiet community tanks where its incessant digging may not be appreciated. (Its former genus name was *Hoplosterum*.)
FEEDING: Carnivore. Will accept a wide variety of commercial meaty catfish foods in the aquarium, such as flakes, pellets and sinking wafers with shrimp, as well as live and frozen foods like bloodworms and *Tubifex* worms. Eagerly accepts chopped earthworms. Feed first thing in the morning and just after the lights go out at night.
HABITAT: Prefers a planted tank with subdued lighting and lots of open swimming areas. Provide a fine-grained substrate that allows for digging without damaging the barbels. Include lots of driftwood, rocks and inverted flowerpots for hiding.
AQUARIUM CARE/BEHAVIOR: May eat small fishes and also becomes aggressive during spawning.
BREEDING: Males develop a blue-violet sheen on their bellies, and orange-colored pectoral spines (see photo above) and build a bubblenest at the surface of the water. Male tends the nest and eggs, and then the young until they are free swimming.

"PIM" ANGELICUS *Pimelodus pictus*
(Pictus Cat, Polka-dot Catfish, Angelica Pim)

MAXIMUM LENGTH: 4 in. (10 cm).

NATIVE RANGE: Northern South America.

MINIMUM AQUARIUM SIZE: 30 gal. (114 L).

GENERAL SWIMMING LEVEL: Bottom to midwater.

OVERVIEW: The "Pim" is a striking silver and black catfish with a wide mouth and long, flowing barbels. It is an active schooling catfish and reportedly pines away if not kept in groups in the aquarium. It will also happily eat small fish it encounters and is thus suited to a community of larger species.

FEEDING: Carnivore. In the wild, feeds on small fishes, insect larvae, assorted aquatic crustaceans and other invertebrates. Provide a diet of more meaty commercial catfish fare, such as flakes, sinking wafers with shrimp, and live and frozen bloodworms, brine shrimp and white worms. They eagerly accept chopped earthworms. Feed first thing in the morning and just after the lights out at night.

HABITAT: *Pimelodus pictus* prefers a tank that is densely planted but with ample open space in the center and strong filtration to create water movement. Gravel should be fine grained and smooth.

AQUARIUM CARE/BEHAVIOR: The "Pim" is a popular aquarium fish because it is so active. When kept in groups of at least three, this nocturnal catfish will be seen swimming in the open during the day. Maintain with larger fishes, as smaller fishes may be eaten. Use only nets with a tight weave to capture these fishes, as they have sharp spines that may be damaged or injure the aquarist.

BREEDING: Not known in the aquarium.

BUSHYNOSE PLECO *Ancistrus* spp.
(Bristlenose Catfish)

MAXIMUM LENGTH: 4 in. (10 cm), for most species.
NATIVE RANGE: Widespread in South America.
MINIMUM AQUARIUM SIZE: 30 gal. (114 L).
GENERAL SWIMMING LEVEL: Bottom.
OVERVIEW: Bushynose Plecos are definite eyecatchers in the aquarium and are showy members of the family *Loricariidae*, armored catfishes with mouths adapted for sucking algae loose from leaves and other substrates. Males have big bushes on their noses, while females have only a few small growths around the rims of their heads. There are many color variations.
FEEDING: Omnivore. These are prodigious algae eaters in the wild but also eat small invertebrates. Will accept a variety of commercial fare designed for catfishes, including flakes and sinking algae wafers, as well as vegetable matter.
HABITAT: Will not generally bother plants in the aquarium. Provide a tank with a fine-grade or rounded gravel substrate for the fish to root in, as well as driftwood and smooth stones for hiding and grazing.
AQUARIUM CARE/BEHAVIOR: The Bushynose Pleco is a peaceful species that can be included in a community setting with a variety of peaceful midwater and top swimmers. Strong filtration and frequent partial water changes are a must, as this species produces lots of waste.
BREEDING: Deposits large clusters of eggs in crevices or hollows of roots. Males guard and fan eggs. Easily raised fry hatch in around five days with attached yolk sac and stay in male's care.

CLOWN PLECO *Panaque maccus*

MAXIMUM LENGTH: 3.5 in. (9 cm).

NATIVE RANGE: Northern South America.

MINIMUM AQUARIUM SIZE: 30 gal. (114 L).

GENERAL SWIMMING LEVEL: Bottom and on substrate.

OVERVIEW: The Clown Pleco is a perfect species for those looking for a smaller loricariid-type catfish to help keep algal growth at bay. It has efficient, scraper-like teeth to rasp algae from wood and rocks and will fit nicely into most community aquariums.

FEEDING: Omnivore. The Clown Pleco does best on a herbivorous diet that includes any of the commercial vegetable-based dry, pelleted or sinking algae wafers designed specifically for catfishes, as well as fresh vegetable matter, such as well-rinsed Romaine lettuce, parboiled zucchini or shell-less peas (see Foods and Feeding for tips on how to "sink" the veggies). Feed first thing in the morning and just after the lights are turned off at night.

HABITAT: Prefers a tank with driftwood for browsing, as well as plenty of caves for hiding or spawning, such as rocks and inverted flowerpots. Live or artificial plants are not a necessity, but can be included as part of the decor. Provide a dark substrate of fine, rounded gravel.

AQUARIUM CARE/BEHAVIOR: The Clown Pleco is a relatively peaceful community tank resident that can be kept with a variety of mid- to top-water swimming species, such as larger tetras. Although they may occasionally defend their territories against conspecifics and even other species, little or no harm is done.

BREEDING: Spawns in caves. Male guards/cares for eggs and young.

LEOPARD PLECO *Pterygoplichthys gibbiceps*
(Sailfin Pleco)

MAXIMUM LENGTH: 12 in. (30 cm).
NATIVE RANGE: Northern South America.
MINIMUM AQUARIUM SIZE: 30 gal. (114 L).
GENERAL SWIMMING LEVEL: Bottom.
OVERVIEW: A lovely catfish that only gets more attractive with age, the Leopard Pleco grows quite large and when seen in the aquarium with its high sail-like dorsal fin fully displayed, it is a truly breathtaking sight. This is a generally peaceful species that can be kept in a community tank with medium to large fish, including cichlids. It may be aggressive toward conspecifics and similar looking species. (Some references place this species in the genus *Glytoperichthys*.)
FEEDING: Omnivore. Like all pleco-type fishes, it will accept a wide variety of commercial vegetable-based catfish foods, including sinking algae wafers, pellets and *Spirulina* flakes, as well as prepared garden vegetables. Feed first thing in the morning and just after the lights go out at night. Will eat small invertebrates if available.
HABITAT: Prefers a tank with lots of hiding places in the form of driftwood or inverted flowerpots. Plants are not a necessity, as they may eat them. This species produces copious amounts of waste and will need heavy filtration and frequent gravel vacuuming.
AQUARIUM CARE/BEHAVIOR: Because it is so attractive and commercially bred, the Leopard Pleco is a popular and readily available aquarium fish. The aquarist may want to obtain a group of 2-3 small individuals to enjoy this wonderful pleco.
BREEDING: Not seen in the aquarium, but males tend eggs and fry.

PLECOSTOMUS *Hypostomus* spp.

MAXIMUM LENGTH: 12 in. (30 cm).

NATIVE RANGE: Throughout South America.

MINIMUM AQUARIUM SIZE: 30 gal. (114 L).

GENERAL SWIMMING LEVEL: Bottom.

OVERVIEW: One of the quintessential aquarium fishes, the pleco is a good beginner's catfish that will survive a wide range of water conditions. Like other loricariid catfishes, they have bony plates instead of scales and a characteristic disk-shaped mouth that enables them to attach firmly to boulders in fast-flowing streams. The former genus name *Plecostomus* is no longer valid, replaced by *Hypostomus*.

FEEDING: Omnivore. The Pleco thrives on herbivorous foods, such as *Spirulina* flakes and sinking algae wafers, as well as well-rinsed Romaine lettuce and parboiled zucchini. Feed first thing in the morning and just after lights-out time in the evening.

HABITAT: Prefers an aquarium with moderately dense vegetation and hiding places in the form of driftwood and inverted flowerpots to refuge in during the day. Acrylic tanks are not recommended, as the Pleco may scratch the panes with its mouth. It can be tough on plants, so use artificial plants instead of live. Unless there is heavy filtration and frequent water changes, the tank will be "adorned" with the long, stringy waste of this species.

AQUARIUM CARE/BEHAVIOR: Although the Pleco may be territorial with its own kind, it is otherwise peaceful and can be kept in a community setting.

BREEDING: Known only in outdoor ponds, as these fishes make and occupy muddy tunnels in which to spawn.

STRIPED RAPHAEL *Platydoras armatulus*
(Striped Raphael, Humbug Catfish, Chocolate Talking Catfish)

MAXIMUM LENGTH: 8.5 in. (22 cm).
NATIVE RANGE: Northern South America.
MINIMUM AQUARIUM SIZE: 20 gal. (76 L).
GENERAL SWIMMING LEVEL: Bottom.
OVERVIEW: The Raphael Catfish is a handsome fish with interesting burrowing behaviors. It needs to be kept with larger fishes or it will pick off smaller tankmates in its nocturnal hunting rounds. Its stout pectoral fin spines can inflict a painful wound and may lock into the open position and are easily caught up in nets (use tight weave net). Handle with care. (The Raphael does not talk, but can grind its pectoral bones in their sockets to produce a noise.)
FEEDING: Carnivore. Provide meaty catfish fare, including flakes, pellets and sinking wafers with shrimp, as well as live and frozen foods. They love snails and will consume them with relish, shells and all. Feed first thing in the morning and at lights-out time.
HABITAT: This species likes to burrow in the sand during the day, so provide a fine-grade or rounded gravel substrate. In nature, they hide among plant cover and hollows of roots, so include plenty of hiding places. Will not bother plants, although the plants may become covered in silt from the Raphael's constant digging.
AQUARIUM CARE/BEHAVIOR: If keeping more than one Raphael Catfish in the aquarium, they may squabble with one another and even similar catfish over the best hiding spots and could do damage with their pectoral fin spines. Keep only with fishes of similar size.
BREEDING: No aquarium cases reported.

CATFISH • PEACEFUL

CUCKOO CATFISH *Synodontis multipunctatus*
(Cuckoo Synodontis, Multi-Spotted Catfish)

MAXIMUM LENGTH: 10 in. (25 cm).

NATIVE RANGE: Lake Tanganyika.

MINIMUM AQUARIUM SIZE: 30 gal. (114 L).

GENERAL SWIMMING LEVEL: Bottom.

OVERVIEW: This is one of the most popular of the *Synodontis* catfishes, a group of immensely likeable, peaceful species that put on a continuous show when kept in groups. Recently, a very similar and co-existing species, *S. grandiops*, has been described. It is smaller (6 in.; 15 cm) and has a much larger eye than *S. multipunctatus*.

FEEDING: Carnivore. In the wild, often feed heavily on snails and will do the same in the aquarium. Accept a wide range of aquarium fare, including tablets, pellets, and flakes. In addition, live and frozen foods, such as brine shrimp and bloodworms, are appreciated. Feed in the morning and at lights-out time at night.

HABITAT: Provide lots of caves, and include fine-grade or rounded gravel substrate. Plants are optional.

AQUARIUM CARE/BEHAVIOR: Generally peaceful. Keep in groups of at least three. *Synodontis* catfishes are perfect tankmates for African Rift Lake Cichlids, as well as larger tetras and other characins.

BREEDING: Known for unusual spawning behavior. Seeks out mouthbrooding cichlids that are spawning, and lays its own eggs among cichlid eggs. Female cichlid scoops up all eggs in her mouth and cares for catfish brood along with her own. When the young catfish hatch in the cichlid's mouth, they feed on the cichlid eggs and newly hatched young.

BIGEYE SYNODONTIS CATFISH
Synodontis alberti
Length: 8 in. (20 cm)

BUGEYE SYNODONTIS CATFISH
Synodontis contractus
Length: 4 in. (10 cm)

CONGICUS SYNODONTIS CATFISH
Synodontis congicus
Length: 8 in. (20 cm)

FEATHERFIN SYNODONTIS CATFISH
Synodontis eupterus
Length: 10 in. (25 cm)

MARBLED SYNODONTIS CATFISH
Synodontis schoutedeni
Length: 6.6 in. (17 cm).

ORANGESTRIPED SYNODONTIS CATFISH
Synodontis flavitaeniatus
Length: 8 in. (20 cm)

UPSIDE-DOWN CATFISH *Synodontis nigriventris*

MAXIMUM LENGTH: Males 3.75 in. (9.5 cm), females slightly larger.

NATIVE RANGE: Lower Congo River, Africa.

MINIMUM AQUARIUM SIZE: 30 gal. (114 L).

GENERAL SWIMMING LEVEL: Typically bottom to mid-water, but top when floating foods are offered.

OVERVIEW: A wonderful little curiosity, this schooling species lives a great part of its life upside down in caves or racing to the surface to feed. Most fishes have lighter-colored bellies to escape predators from below, while these fish live an inverted lifestyle and are darker on the ventral side and lighter on top to avoid predators from above.

FEEDING: Omnivore. The Upside-down Catfish will accept a wide variety of meaty catfish fare, including good-quality flakes, tablets, sinking wafers, as well as live and frozen bloodworms, brine shrimp and *Daphnia*. Also offer vegetable-based foods like *Spirulina* flakes and sinking algae wafers. Feed first thing in the morning and just after the lights go out at night.

HABITAT: Prefers a tank planted with broad-leaved plants, such as *Echinodorus* spp. Needs a layer of floating plants or some other overhanging retreats under which to conceal itself. Choice of substrate is not important. Decorate with driftwood, as well as PVC piping to create tunnels for possible spawning.

AQUARIUM CARE/BEHAVIOR: The Upside-down Catfish is a peaceful species that should be kept in groups of at least three with other relatively mild-mannered community tank residents.

BREEDING: Rarely bred in the aquarium. There are indications that there might be some degree of parental care of the eggs.

ZAMORA CATFISH *Auchenipterichthys coracoideus*
(Midnight Catfish, Zamora Wood Cat)

MAXIMUM LENGTH: 5 in. (13 cm).
NATIVE RANGE: Northern South America.
MINIMUM AQUARIUM SIZE: 30 gal. (114 L).
GENERAL SWIMMING LEVEL: Bottom.
OVERVIEW: This odd-looking catfish is one of the "Driftwood or Wood Cats," a name derived from its favorite hiding places in the wild, where it refuges in groups. It sports a peculiar long cranial 'shield,' which gives the impression that the dorsal fin starts at the neck. Ideally, it should be kept in groups of at least three (the more the better), which will make it more comfortable in the aquarium and more apt to eat.
FEEDING: Carnivore. The Zamora Catfish feeds on insects, insect larvae and small crustaceans in the wild, and will accept a wide variety of commercial meaty fare in the aquarium, including good-quality flakes, pellets and sinking wafers. Supplement with live or frozen foods, such as bloodworms and *Tubifex* worms. Feed first thing in the morning and just after the lights go out at night.
HABITAT: This species prefers a tank with subdued lighting (provide a layer of floating plants) and lots of hiding places in the form of driftwood, rocks and inverted flowerpots in which it can hide during the day. Strong filtration and regular water changes a must.
AQUARIUM CARE/BEHAVIOR: The Zamora Catfish is nocturnal and may seem reclusive at first. Once it becomes accustomed to the tank and feeding schedule, it will spend more time in the open.
BREEDING: Internally fertilizing egglayer with no known parental care.

AFRICAN BUTTERFLY CICHLID *Anomalochromis thomasi*
(Thomas's Dwarf Cichlid)

MAXIMUM LENGTH: 3 in. (8 cm), females smaller.
NATIVE RANGE: West Africa.
MINIMUM AQUARIUM SIZE: 20 gal. (76 L).
GENERAL SWIMMING LEVEL: Bottom.
OVERVIEW: This is a lovely dwarf cichlid, with all the behaviors that make this family perennial favorites among aquarists of all skill levels. They are fish with personalities and highly developed breeding behaviors. The African Butterfly Cichlid is a peaceful fish well suited to life in a smaller aquarium.
FEEDING: Omnivore. In the wild, this species feeds mainly on insect larvae and algae. In the aquarium, it will accept most prepared foods, including flakes, frozen and freeze-dried foods, two to three times daily. Color-enhancing foods containing carotene will help to bring out the rosy background color and red spotting.
HABITAT: In the wild, this species inhabits clear rivers in wooded and bushy areas and will prefer a heavily planted tank with hiding places in the form of rocks, driftwood and inverted flowerpots, with plenty of open areas for swimming. A dark substrate will help to show off its colors. Provide flat stones as spawning sites.
AQUARIUM CARE/BEHAVIOR: This is a peaceful species that forms strong pair bonds and is territorial, especially during spawning. House with peaceful, schooling species that are top swimmers, as well as cave spawners, such as *Pelvicachromis* spp.
BREEDING: Deposits eggs on flat rocks or plants. Fry guarded by both parents. Difficult to distinguish the sexes.

AGASSIZ'S DWARF CICHLID *Apistogramma agassizii*
(Agassazii)

MAXIMUM LENGTH: Males 3 in. (7.5 cm), Females 1.5 in. (3.75 cm).
NATIVE RANGE: Backwaters of the Peruvian and Brazilian Amazon.
MINIMUM AQUARIUM SIZE: 5 gal. (19 L).
GENERAL SWIMMING LEVEL: Bottom to midwater.
OVERVIEW: *A. agassizii* is truly a spectacular-looking dwarf cichlid. For authenticity, acquire one male to several females and let them pair up or establish a harem—each female will establish a territory to be visited by the male. Several geographic populations and color varieties are available.
FEEDING: Carnivore. In the wild, these fish pick at small invertebrates, such as insect larvae and worms that live in the substrate and leaf litter. Although there are now many commercial cichlid foods on the market designed specifically for them, they don't do well solely on prepared foods and must have live and frozen foods to thrive.
HABITAT: Keep them in soft, acidic water that has been filtered over peat or with blackwater extract added. They do best in a well-planted tank with Java Fern or Java Moss anchored to driftwood, and floating plants, with plenty of hiding places such as driftwood or inverted flowerpots to provide each female her own domain. Use a fine-grade gravel substrate.
AQUARIUM CARE/BEHAVIOR: Agassiz' Dwarf Cichlid is moderately territorial, more so when breeding events are taking place. Peaceful, mid-water schooling dither fishes like tetras will make them feel more secure. Good water quality is a must.
BREEDING: Cave spawners. Females care for the brood.

ANGELFISH *Pterophyllum scalare*

MAXIMUM LENGTH: 8 in. tall x 6 in. long (20 x 15 cm).

NATIVE RANGE: Rio Negro, Amazon, including Guyana, Peru and Brazil, also widely bred commercially.

MINIMUM AQUARIUM SIZE: 30 gal. (110 L) high for a pair.

GENERAL SWIMMING LEVEL: Entire tank.

OVERVIEW: The stately and ever-graceful Angelfish is an icon of the aquarium hobby, even recognized by non-aquarists. They are available in many forms and fin types, as they are quite genetically malleable. They are generally sold quite young, as small as a dime, and this can lead to trouble as a pair of mature angelfish can quite dominate the aquarium and efficiently pick off all the small tetras and other prey they can catch and swallow.

FEEDING: Carnivore. *P. scalare* is a voracious feeder that will accept a wide variety of frozen and prepared foods.

HABITAT: Angelfish prefer a high tank that is well planted around the sides and back. *Sagittaria*, *Vallisneria* and driftwood are classic in the angelfish aquarium.

AQUARIUM CARE/BEHAVIOR: Angelfish live in peaceful schools when young, but pair off at about 9 months of age, after which the pairs typically become quite territorial and aggressive. From this point on they should only be kept with fishes that will not interfere with their spawning activities. A single specimen, however, is quite versatile in community settings.

BREEDING: Angelfish deposit the eggs on a vertical surface in the aquarium, such as a plant leaf or the glass walls. Both the male and female tend the eggs and guard the fry for a time.

BLACK LACE ANGEL
Pterophyllum scalare
Height: 8 in. (20 cm)

BLACK LACE VEIL ANGEL
Pterophyllum scalare
Height: 8 in. (20 cm)

BLUE-BLACK ANGELFISH
Pterophyllum scalare
Height: 8 in. (20 cm)

GOLD ANGELFISH
Pterophyllum scalare
Height: 8 in. (20 cm)

HALF-BLACK ANGELFISH
Pterophyllum scalare
Height: 8 in. (20 cm)

MARBLE ANGELFISH
Pterophyllum scalare
Height: 8 in. (20 cm)

BLUE ACARA *Aequidens pulcher*

MAXIMUM LENGTH: 6-8 in. (15-20 cm).

NATIVE RANGE: Northwestern South America and the coastal regions of Venezuela, including the island of Trinidad, down to the Orinoco River.

MINIMUM AQUARIUM SIZE: 40 gal. (150 L.) for full-size adults.

GENERAL SWIMMING LEVEL: Mid-water and bottom dwellers.

OVERVIEW: This is a wonderful beginner's cichlid. The Blue Acara is a lovely fish, generally peaceful, that takes on spectacular colors when mature and in breeding form. Several other species, including *A. latifrons*, *A. coeruleopunctuatus* and *A. sapayensis*, are also sold as "blue acaras," and all will require similar care.

FEEDING: Carnivore. Like the Convict Cichlid, the Blue Acara will accept just about any food item that comes its way. Feed a varied diet of any of the commercial cichlid pelleted or flake foods, as well as freeze-dried, frozen and live foods, such as bloodworms, brine shrimp and krill.

HABITAT: The Blue Acara prefers an aquarium with a dark gravel substrate, and several rocks and driftwood to provide hiding places and for spawning. Does best with a regimen of regular water changes.

AQUARIUM CARE/BEHAVIOR: Territorial—acquire one male to several females. Definite sexual dimorphism: males are substantially larger and have longer fins.

BREEDING: Typical of many cichlids, they are bi-parental substrate spawners that lay adhesive eggs primarily on rocks. Pairs form monogamous bonds. Females are slightly rounder.

BRICHARDI *Neolamprologus brichardi*
(Princess of Burundi, Fairy Cichlid, Brichard's Lyretail Cichlid)

MAXIMUM LENGTH: 3.5 in. (9 cm).

NATIVE RANGE: Rocky shoreline of Lake Tanganyika.

MINIMUM AQUARIUM SIZE: 30 gal. (76-114 L) long.

GENERAL SWIMMING LEVEL: Bottom to midwater.

OVERVIEW: The Brichardi is a sleek, elongate fish with stunning coloration and delicate fin filaments. It is one of the easiest of the Tanganyikan cichlids to keep and a good beginner's African cichlid.

FEEDING: Carnivore. Picks at small crustaceans and invertebrates in the wild. In the aquarium, it will accept a wide variety of meaty prepared foods. Supplement with live and frozen foods, such as brine shrimp, mysid shrimp or *Cyclops*.

HABITAT: African cichlids love rocks, rocks and more rocks. In the wild, they inhabit caves in the lake or live in tunnels dug under rocks. A tank for the Brichardi must include a jumble of rocks to form caves and, because they need hard, alkaline water, a dolomite or coral-based gravel substrate. Rockwork must be firmly anchored as these fish are diggers that may topple rock structures, damaging the tank or themselves. Plants may be included, although they are subject to uprooting by the cichlids.

AQUARIUM CARE/BEHAVIOR: This species should be kept in groups of at least three. It is highly territorial—for best results, keep larger tankmates and add before the cichlids.

BREEDING: Pair-forming cave spawner. In some cases, a male may spawn with more than one female. A compatible pair spawns regularly and the young will assist in the rearing of subsequent broods.

CICHLID · TERRITORIAL

71

COCKATOO DWARF CICHLID *Apistogramma cacatuoides*
(Crested Dwarf Cichlid)

MAXIMUM LENGTH: Males to 3.5 in. (9 cm), females 1.5 in. (3 cm).

NATIVE RANGE: Peruvian Amazon, also commercially bred.

MINIMUM AQUARIUM SIZE: 10 gal. (19 L), for a pair or trio.

GENERAL SWIMMING LEVEL: Bottom to midwater.

OVERVIEW: Cockatoo Dwarf Cichlids are showy fish, true cichlids in deportment and personality but in a size that fits even small aquariums. They do well in a community setting as long as their territorial boundaries are respected.

FEEDING: Carnivore. Like other members of the genus *Apistogramma*, these cichlids feed on insects, crustaceans and worms in the wild. Tank-raised specimens will accept a variety of small flake and pelleted foods designed for cichlids in the aquarium. Frozen and live foods should also be offered and will help acclimate wild-caught forms.

HABITAT: The Cockatoo Dwarf Cichlid is at home with a dark substrate and several cave-like escapes. The more abundant the hiding places, the more outgoing these little fish will be.

AQUARIUM CARE/BEHAVIOR: *A. cacatuoides* is a species that does best when kept in groups of one male to several females. Mid-water swimming dither fishes like many of the tetras inspire confidence in these somewhat shy fish. The water should be slightly acidic with a pH of 6.5 to 7, and the water temperature between 77-86°F (25-30° C). Regular water changes are necessary.

BREEDING: Cave spawners. One male will spawn with several females, each with its own separate breeding cave or flowerpot.

CONVICT CICHLID *Amatitlania nigrofasciatus*
(Zebra Cichlid)

MAXIMUM LENGTH: Males 4-5 in. (13 cm), females 2-3 in. (8 cm).
NATIVE RANGE: Nicaragua to Costa Rica, also commercially bred.
MINIMUM AQUARIUM SIZE: 20 long or 30 gal. (76-114 L) for a group.
GENERAL SWIMMING LEVEL: Throughout the aquarium.
OVERVIEW: The Convict Cichlid is a beautiful, iridescent cichlid that is very durable and well worth keeping. As long as there is a pair in the aquarium, the fish will spawn. They may be quite aggressive toward other tankmates, especially when nesting, so avoid keeping small or timid fishes with them. (Former genus was *Cryptoheros*.)
FEEDING: *Amatitliana nigrofasciatus* will accept just about any fish food offered. Feed a varied diet of the commercial cichlid foods available, as well as frozen foods, such as bloodworms, krill, whiteworms and so on.
HABITAT: No matter what the decor, the Convict is always at home. Convict Cichlids should be kept in a well-filtered aquarium with a few flat rocks and a cave or two. Plants are not a necessity, as these fish will be particularly hard on them. Include only artificial plants or plants potted in flowerpots buried in the substrate.
AQUARIUM CARE/BEHAVIOR: The Convict Cichlid is a hardy species that can adapt to just about any water conditions, which is why it's such a good beginner's cichlid.
BREEDING: Biparental substrate and cave spawner. A tank devoted to a pair will allow the aquarist to observe their fascinating breeding behaviors, including the rearing of the fry.

FINLEY'S CICHLID *Benitochromis finleyi*

MAXIMUM LENGTH: 4 in. (10 cm).

NATIVE RANGE: West Africa.

MINIMUM AQUARIUM SIZE: 30 gal. (114 L).

GENERAL SWIMMING LEVEL: Bottom.

OVERVIEW: Here is a character, feisty and full of typical African cichlid spunk, but in a manageable size. *Benitochromis finleyi* is characterized by iridescent blue coloration on the cheeks, operculum and anterior portion of the body. Males are larger with a dorsal fin trimmed in red.

FEEDING: Carnivore. This species will accept a variety of commercial meaty fare, including cichlid flakes and pelleted foods, as well as freeze-dried, frozen and live foods like bloodworms and brine shrimp.

HABITAT: Finley's Cichlid is a substrate-sifting cichlid that will require a tank with a fine-grade or rounded-gravel substrate with lots of open swimming room, and plenty of rocks and inverted flowerpots in which to hide. They generally do not uproot live plants, although they may dislodge roots during their normal foraging activities. Strong filtration and regular water changes are a must.

AQUARIUM CARE/BEHAVIOR: Finley's Cichlid is moderately tolerant of its own kind, except during spawning, but is generally peaceful with similar-size fishes. Purchase a group of juveniles and let them pair up. However, individual pairs may become aggressive toward other species and will probably need to be relocated to their own tanks later on.

BREEDING: This is a biparental mouthbrooder that practices long-term defense of their fry.

FIREMOUTH *Thorichthys meeki*

MAXIMUM LENGTH: 6 in. (15 cm).
NATIVE RANGE: Mexico and Guatemala.
MINIMUM AQUARIUM SIZE: 29 gal. (110 L).
GENERAL SWIMMING LEVEL: Bottom.
OVERVIEW: The Firemouth is a very distinctive cichlid, known best for its impressive red-throated gill-flaring defensive display and fierce parental instincts. Although they are territorial, they will rarely bother tankmates unless they are spawning, in which case they may be aggressive toward smaller conspecifics. They are best kept with other fishes of similar size and temperament.
FEEDING: Carnivore. Not a particularly fussy eater, it will accept a wide variety of commercial cichlid fare, including flakes, pelleted and stick foods, as well as live and frozen foods.
HABITAT: The Firemouth is a substrate-sifting species that prefers an aquarium with a fine-grade gravel substrate and plenty of hiding places in the form of rock caves or inverted flowerpots. Spawning is virtually inevitable when there is a pair of Firemouths in an aquarium that has a flat rock and a cave. Provide plenty of open areas in the center for swimming. They are know to dig, so be sure that all structures in the aquarium are safely situated.
AQUARIUM CARE/BEHAVIOR: The Firemouth is relatively easy to keep in the aquarium, as it will tolerate, and is forgiving of, a wide range of water conditions. Must have a regimen of regular water changes, or it may bloat.
BREEDING: Firemouths are bi-parental substrate spawners that make excellent parents. The fry are protected in pits in the substrate.

FLAG CICHLID *Laetacara curviceps*
(Smiling Acara)

MAXIMUM LENGTH: Males to 3 in. (7.5 cm), females smaller.

NATIVE RANGE: Northwestern South America.

MINIMUM AQUARIUM SIZE: 15-20 gal. (57-76 L).

GENERAL SWIMMING LEVEL: Bottom to midwater.

OVERVIEW: This is a true dwarf acara that is great for a small community aquarium. Their bodies are typically chunky and the blue markings near their mouths give rise to their alternate common name: Smiling Acara.

FEEDING: Carnivore. Tank-raised specimens will accept almost any of the commercially prepared foods, including cichlid flakes and pellets, but wild-caught forms will initially require live foods, such as well-cleaned blackworms, frozen bloodworms, etc., after which they can be gradually acclimated to prepared foods.

HABITAT: Provide a densely planted—anchored and floating—aquarium, with lots of hiding places (rocks, PVC piping, driftwood and inverted flowerpots), as the more hiding places these cichlids have, the more you will see them out in the open. Warm (76-84°F; 24-29°C) and well-filtered water required.

AQUARIUM CARE/BEHAVIOR: They are relatively peaceful, but may become somewhat aggressive during spawning. Provide dither fishes like small, schooling tetras to make them more comfortable.

BREEDING: Bi-parental substrate spawners, in which both male and female participate in the selection and cleaning of a suitable site. Acquire a group of four to six and let them pair up.

GOLD OCELLATUS *Lamprologus ocellatus*
(Shell-dwelling Lamp, Red Ocellatus)

MAXIMUM LENGTH: Male 2 in. (5 cm), female 1.5 in. (3.5 cm).
NATIVE RANGE: Lake Tanganyika.
MINIMUM AQUARIUM SIZE: 20 gal. (76 L).
GENERAL SWIMMING LEVEL: Bottom.
OVERVIEW: *Lamprologus ocellatus* is a fascinating and beautiful dwarf cichlid from Africa that possesses outstanding behavioral and reproductive characteristics. There is a beautiful gold variant available, as well as blue and purple variants and a yellow-finned variety.
FEEDING: Carnivore. These fishes are relatively unfinicky and will accept most commercial cichlid foods, as well as small live foods, such as brine shrimp and bloodworms.
HABITAT: This is a shell dweller that will need large snail shells, at least one per fish, to hide in and among. A male fish will defend its snail shell against all other fish, regardless of their size. Shells sold for hermit crabs in pet stores will do quite well—"escargot" shells sold in supermarkets will need to be boiled and cleaned before use. They need hard, alkaline water to thrive, so provide a dolomite or coral-based gravel substrate that is fine-grade (not coarse, as they may bury their shells, leaving only the openings visible). Plant sparsely on the sides and back of the aquarium and keep other decor like rocks restricted to these areas as well.
AQUARIUM CARE/BEHAVIOR: Keep only one male to several females. This is a great fish for a Lake Tanganyika community.
BREEDING: Demersal (snail shell) spawner that will lay eggs in the snail shell normally occupied by the female.

GOLDEN JULIE *Julidochromis ornatus*
(Yellow Julie, Ornate Julie)

MAXIMUM LENGTH: 3.3 in. (8.5 cm).

NATIVE RANGE: Rocky Coast of Lake Tanganyika.

MINIMUM AQUARIUM SIZE: 20 gal. (76 L).

GENERAL SWIMMING LEVEL: Bottom.

OVERVIEW: The Golden Julie is an especially attractive Dwarf Cichlid with an elongate body, wonderful contrasting coloration and a territorial attitude that African cichlid enthusiasts find fascinating and admirable.

FEEDING: Omnivore. Not a picky eater, this species will accept a wide range of live, frozen and prepared meaty foods in the aquarium, including cichlid flakes and granules that contain vegetable matter. Color-enhancing foods containing carotene will help in maintaining this fish's rich yellow color pigments.

HABITAT: Like other Rift Lake cichlids, this species requires hard, alkaline water that is best provided by including a dolomite or coral-based gravel substrate. An efficient biological filter is also essential, as *Julidochromis* spp. are extremely sensitive to poor water quality. It prefers a tank with lots of stable rockwork to form numerous caves and a few hardy plants, such as *Vallisneria*.

AQUARIUM CARE/BEHAVIOR: Purchase several and let them pair up. Pairs are highly territorial and extremely intolerant of conspecifics and other Dwarf Julies.

BREEDING: Julies are biparental cave spawners that form strong pair bonds. Multiple generations of young can peacefully coexist in the same aquarium.

GUENTHER'S MOUTHBROODER *Chromidotilapia guentheri*

MAXIMUM LENGTH: 6.2 in. (16 cm).

NATIVE RANGE: West and Central Africa.

MINIMUM AQUARIUM SIZE: 30 gal. (114 L).

GENERAL SWIMMING LEVEL: Bottom.

OVERVIEW: Here is an attractive African cichlid with subtle beauty and fascinating mouthbrooding habits. It is relatively peaceful with other bigger, self-assured species, but is not safe with small, mild-mannered fishes.

FEEDING: Omnivore. Guenther's Mouthbrooder is relatively easy to feed and will accept a wide variety of meaty aquarium fare, including good-quality cichlid pellets, sticks and flakes, as well as freeze-dried and frozen foods like krill, *Mysis* shrimp and bloodworms. Supplement with foods rich in plant matter, such as *Spirulina*-based foods.

HABITAT: Because these are substrate-sifting fishes, they will need a tank with a fine-grade gravel substrate and lots of hiding places among driftwood and piles of well-anchored rocks to form numerous caves for adults, and nooks and crannies for fry and juveniles to hide in.

AQUARIUM CARE/BEHAVIOR: Guenther's Mouthbrooder is an active species that is generally compatible with other fishes of similar size and temperament. It may be aggressive toward its own kind during spawning and have a distinct pecking order. The best approach is to purchase a group of juveniles and let them pair up.

BREEDING: This species forms pairs, with the male doing mouthbrooding duties. Later both parents take care of the young.

KRIB *Pelvicachromis pulcher*
(Kribensis, Rainbow Krib, Purple Cichlid)

MAXIMUM LENGTH: 4 in. (10 cm).
NATIVE RANGE: West Africa, most commercially bred.
MINIMUM AQUARIUM SIZE: 20 gal. (76 L).
GENERAL SWIMMING LEVEL: Bottom.
OVERVIEW: Long a favorite among dwarf-cichlid buffs, the Krib is a beautiful fish of modest size that is relatively easy to keep. Males have long extensions to the dorsal and anal fins. Females develop a deep pink to purple belly when spawning. Available in a variety of colors, including an albino. Its popular common name derives from the species' previous scientific label, *Pelmatochromis kribensis*.
FEEDING: Omnivore. Not a picky eater, the Krib will accept a wide variety of commercial fare, including cichlid flake or pelleted foods. Also provide freeze-dried, frozen and live foods, such as brine shrimp, black worms and bloodworms. *Spirulina* and color-enhancing foods will also be accepted.
HABITAT: The Krib prefers a densely planted aquarium, with rocky caves or inverted flowerpots. Use a dark fine-grade substrate to best show off their colors.
AQUARIUM CARE/BEHAVIOR: Forms pairs and is relatively peaceful, except during spawning. Acquire one male to several females and let them pair up. Can be kept in a community setting, but care should be taken in choosing tankmakes. Avoid keeping with other cave dwellers.
BREEDING: Pair forming cave spawners. Female guards the eggs and later both parents care for the fry.

MARLIER'S JULIE *Julidochromis marlieri*

MAXIMUM LENGTH: 5 in. (13 cm).

NATIVE RANGE: Rocky Coast of Lake Tanganyika.

MINIMUM AQUARIUM SIZE: 30 gal. (114 L).

GENERAL SWIMMING LEVEL: Bottom.

OVERVIEW: These are strikingly colored fish with a facial structure many find comical or endearing. They are generally more peaceful than many African cichlids but very scrappy with their own kind. Although there is variation among populations, these fish are typically seen with a black and white checkerboard-type pattern. Older males often show some humping to their head area. The mouth is larger than that seen in *J. ornatus*.

FEEDING: Omnivore. Like other members of the genus, *Julidochromis marlieri* is not a particularly fussy eater and will accept a wide range of live, frozen and prepared meaty foods in the aquarium, including cichlid flakes. Some herbivore and color-enhancing rations should be fed regularly.

HABITAT: Marlier's Julie prefers a tank with lots of rock formations in which to hide, as well as a few hardy plants. Rockwork should be well anchored to prevent toppling. Because they need hard, alkaline water, provide a dolomite or coral-based substrate.

AQUARIUM CARE/BEHAVIOR: Start with a small group and let them pair up. These are territorial cichlids that may be intolerant toward conspecifics.

BREEDING: Marlier's Cichlids are cave spawners that lay their eggs on the ceilings of caves. They form pair bonds and both parents guard the spawn. It is difficult to distinguish the sexes.

OSCAR *Astronotus ocellatus*

MAXIMUM LENGTH: 12-14 in. (30-36 cm)

NATIVE RANGE: Amazon and Orinoco basins, northern Paraguay, also commercially bred.

MINIMUM AQUARIUM SIZE: 55 gal. (209 L).

GENERAL SWIMMING LEVEL: Throughout the aquarium.

OVERVIEW: This "personality fish" is one of the best-known cichlids. It may live for 10-plus years, and will interact more and more with its owner over time. Several color and finnage variations available.

FEEDING: Long thought to be the "food of choice" for *A. ocellatus*, live feeder fish are not necessary to keep your Oscar healthy and alert. Does best on a variety of foods specifically designed for omnivorous cichlids. Supplement with freeze-dried krill for adults, bloodworms for juveniles.

HABITAT: Oscars are prone to "rearranging" their tanks, so care should be taken when setting up the decor. Provide several rock piles (preferably anchored in place to avoid toppling, and not near the glass) throughout the tank in which they can hide. Any plants should be potted and buried in the substrate, floating or anchored to driftwood (Java fern, Java moss). Deep gravel substrate is preferred.

AQUARIUM CARE/BEHAVIOR: Oscars are generally peaceful, despite their size. Acquire four or more young individuals in as large a tank as possible. Heavy filtration and frequent partial water changes are a must, as these are messy eaters. Lax attention to water quality may lead to "Hole-in-the-Head" disease.

BREEDING: Oscars form cohesive pairs and spawn in the open, often in pits dug in the gravel.

PEACOCK CICHLID *Aulonocara jacobfreibergi*
(Malawi Butterfly Cichlid)

MAXIMUM LENGTH: 6 in. (15 cm).

NATIVE RANGE: Rocky shorelines, usually near sandy areas in Lake Malawi.

MINIMUM AQUARIUM SIZE: 30-40 gal. (114-152 L).

GENERAL SWIMMING LEVEL: Bottom to midwater.

OVERVIEW: This is one of the classic Malawi Peacocks, brillliantly colored with a swallow's tail and an ideal African cichlid for beginners and for those hobbyists wanting to breed African cichlids for the first time. Extreme differences in coloration exist between populations.

FEEDING: Carnivore. In the wild, the Peacock Cichlid feeds on micro-invertebrates found hidden in the sand, but will readily adapt to a variety of commercially prepared cichlid diets, such as flakes and pellets. Supplement with meaty frozen and freeze-dried foods, such as brine shrimp or black worms. Live foods will be eaten with relish.

HABITAT: The Peacock Cichlid needs both rocky and open swimming areas and is primarily a cave dweller. Provide smooth rocks to form caves and, because they need hard, alkaline water to thrive, lay down a fine-grade dolomite or coral-based gravel substrate. This is a sizable fish that needs room to swim and maneuver.

AQUARIUM CARE/BEHAVIOR: They are generally peaceful, although males may quarrel over females or territory. In the wild, they live in large groups.

BREEDING: Maternal mouthbrooder. Acquire one male to several females to start. Females are much less flamboyantly colored.

MOTHER-OF-PEARL EARTHEATER *Geophagus brasiliensis*
(Brazil Eartheater, Pearl Cichlid, Brasiliensis)

MAXIMUM LENGTH: Males to 10 in. (25 cm), females half to two-thirds that size.

NATIVE RANGE: Southeastern Brazil.

MINIMUM AQUARIUM SIZE: 55 gal. and up (209 L).

GENERAL SWIMMING LEVEL: Bottom to midwater.

OVERVIEW: Defying the usual laws of nature, here is a species that grows more attractive as it ages. Juveniles are unimpressive, but mature into lovely, iridescent adults. They are called eartheaters because they dig in the substrate and sift small insects and worms out of the sand. They are best housed in a larger aquarium with other big cichlids or in a species tank of their own.

FEEDING: Omnivore. This Eartheater will readily accept a varied diet of cichlid foods, as well as live, frozen and freeze-dried foods, such as bloodworms, chopped earthworms and krill.

HABITAT: They need a fine-grade gravel substrate in the aquarium. Include hiding places among rocks and driftwood. Any plants to be included should be hardy and planted in pots buried in the substrate or anchored on driftwood.

AQUARIUM CARE/BEHAVIOR: Territorial. Provide dither fish like larger characins that are fast-swimming midwater residents.

BREEDING: They are typical substrate spawners that make wonderful parents. The male defends the territory, and the female guards the eggs. They can spawn when still small, 2-3 in. (5-7 cm). Male is noticeably larger and develops a pronounced nuchal hump.

PORT CICHLID *Cichlasoma portalegrense*

MAXIMUM LENGTH: 6 in. (15 cm.)

NATIVE RANGE: La Plata Basin, Argentina, southern Brazil.

MINIMUM AQUARIUM SIZE: 40 gal. (150 L).

GENERAL SWIMMING LEVEL: Throughout the aquarium.

OVERVIEW: The Port Cichlid is stately fish, impressive with its high iridescence and beautifully reticulated finnage. It is a hardy species and an excellent choice for the beginner wanting to breed one of the larger cichlids.

FEEDING: Omnivore. It can thrive on meaty prepared foods, but the inclusion of color-enhancing foods, such as freeze-dried krill and *Spirulina*-based foods, frozen bloodworms and chopped earthworms is strongly recommended to bring out their full iridescent colors.

HABITAT: In nature, this species will deposit its eggs on fallen plant leaves that can be moved when threatened by predators. It can be housed in a planted aquarium. Provide lots of hiding places in the form of rocks, inverted flowerpots and driftwood.

AQUARIUM CARE/BEHAVIOR: This is a relatively undemanding cichlid that will do well under good filtration and regular water changes. The Port Cichlid is a territorial, but peaceful, fish that can be combined in a community tank with other acaras, catfish, and smaller fishes in the upper swimming levels. Males may quarrel over territory, although little damage is done.

BREEDING: Port Cichlids are bi-parental substrate spawners that make exemplary parents. Acquire a group of at least four and let them pair up.

RAINBOW CICHLID *Archocentrus multispinosa*

MAXIMUM LENGTH: 4-5 in. (10-13 cm).

NATIVE RANGE: Honduras to Costa Rica.

MINIMUM AQUARIUM SIZE: 15-20 gal. (57-76 L).

GENERAL SWIMMING LEVEL: Bottom to midwater.

OVERVIEW: The Rainbow Cichlid is a popular, not-too-large cichlid that is relatively peaceful and full of personality. Has unique "tricuspid" teeth, which it uses to rasp filamentous algae (a major part of its diet in the wild) from rockwork and other aquarium decor. These three specialized teeth have earned *multispinosa* its own genus, *Herotilapia*.

FEEDING: Omnivore. Because a good portion of the Rainbow Cichlid's diet in the wild is filamentous algae, be sure to provide sufficient plant matter in their diets, including commercial *Spirulina* foods. Also provide a variety of commercial foods designed for cichlids, as well as live, frozen and freeze-dried foods, such as brine shrimp or bloodworms.

HABITAT: It needs a tank with a fine-grade gravel substrate, and lots of hiding places in the form of rocks and roots, or inverted flowerpots. Tends to leave plants alone.

AQUARIUM CARE/BEHAVIOR: *H. multispinosa* is a territorial, but peaceful, cichlid that is rarely aggressive except during spawning. Keep one male to several females, with other fishes of similar size and temperament.

BREEDING: Sexes are easy to distinguish. Lays large numbers of eggs on a clean rock. Fry are guided into pits where the parents guard them.

CICHLID • PEACEFUL

RAM DWARF CICHLID *Microgeophagus ramirezi*
(Butterfly Dwarf, German Blue Ram, Apisto, Mikrogeophagus)

MAXIMUM LENGTH: 2 in. (6 cm).
NATIVE RANGE: Venezuela.
MINIMUM AQUARIUM SIZE: 5 gal. (19 L).
GENERAL SWIMMING LEVEL: Bottom to midwater.
OVERVIEW: One of the best-liked of the dwarf cichlids, the Ram is a gorgeous gold and metallic blue fish with all the spirit and personality of its family. There are several color strains available, including a veiltail variety.
FEEDING: Omnivore. Rams will accept a wide variety of small prepared foods and should also be offered frozen, live and freeze-dried foods, such as bloodworms, brine shrimp, krill and mosquito larvae.
HABITAT: *M. ramirezi* prefers soft, acidic water (pH 6.5) and high temperature (77-86°F or 25-30°C). Because it is extremely sensitive about water quality, perform frequent partial water changes. Prefers an aquarium with lots of cover and open swimming spaces as well. Easily spooked, so place tank in an area with little or no traffic. Provide tank background—painted a dark color or given a scenic background.
AQUARIUM CARE/BEHAVIOR: Small or peaceful tankmates that will tolerate higher temperatures. Acquire one male to several females and let them pair up. Unfortunately, the Ram is relatively short-lived in the aquarium (1-2 years).
BREEDING: The Ram is a monogamous species that forms pair bonds, and spawns in the open, typically on a flat surface. They will vigorously defend their young. (Pair shown above have spawned on a flat rock and are guarding their eggs.)

RED-HUMP EARTHEATER *Geophagus steindachneri*

MAXIMUM LENGTH: Males to 6 in. (15 cm); females half that size.

NATIVE RANGE: Northwestern South America, Colombia.

MINIMUM AQUARIUM SIZE: 30 gal. (115 L) long.

GENERAL SWIMMING LEVEL: Bottom to midwater.

OVERVIEW: Along with the Mother-of-Pearl Eartheater, the Red Hump Eartheater is one of the most easily bred and undemanding of the *Geophagus* species, which exercise fascinating-to-watch mouth-brooding care of their young. The males sport a red nuchal hump on their heads. Several color varieties available.

FEEDING: Omnivore. The Red-Hump Eartheater will readily accept a varied diet consisting of a variety of commercial pelleted, stick or flake cichlid foods, as well as live, frozen and freeze-dried foods, such as bloodworms, earthworms and krill.

HABITAT: Because this species can be belligerent, particularly with conspecifics, it is important to provide lots of shelter. Create hiding places among rocks and driftwood, as well as inverted flowerpots. Plants are optional.

AQUARIUM CARE/BEHAVIOR: The Red-Hump Eartheater is best kept in a group of one male to several females. Because these cichlids are relatively undemanding in terms of their care, they are great beginner's cichlids. They can be housed with other cichlids of similar temperaments or top-swimming characins.

BREEDING: These fish are maternal mouthbrooders; the female broods the eggs in her mouth and tends the fry. (See Breeding, pages 178-183.) Egg-carrying females should be carefully removed to a separate tank to avoid injury.

SEVERUM *Heros notatus* (and other *Heros* spp.)
(Banded Cichlid)

MAXIMUM LENGTH: 10-12 in. (25-30 cm).
NATIVE RANGE: Rio Negro basin, Brazil.
MINIMUM AQUARIUM SIZE: 55 gal. (209 L).
GENERAL SWIMMING LEVEL: Mostly midwater to top.
OVERVIEW: A number of different, but related, cichlids are sold as Severums. To make matters more interesting, there are many color morphs and many color changes based on mood. They can be belligerent but are a good choice for a moderately rowdy cichlid community.
FEEDING: Omnivore. The Severum is a hearty eater that will accept a variety of foods. Its diet should include a variety of plant material (e.g., Romaine lettuce, spinach), in addition to regular prepared pelleted, frozen and live foods, such as bloodworms, earthworms and krill.
HABITAT: Lives in still or slow-moving waters in the wild. The Severum prefers a tank with several flat stones and a cave or two. Plants are optional, although a cover of floating plants like water sprite or *Salvinia* spp., may offer them a quick "snack." Good filtration and regular water changes are a must.
AQUARIUM CARE/BEHAVIOR: Though shy, they are territorial and may become more aggressive during spawning. Pairing is difficult, and the presence of dither fishes may increase chances of pairing.
BREEDING: The Severum is a bi-parental, open spawner that sometimes chooses vertical surfaces in the manner of Angelfish. Forms strong pair bonds and is moderately difficult to breed.

TANGANYIKAN LEMON CICHLID *Neolamprologus leleupi*
(Lemon Yellow Cichlid, Leleupi)

MAXIMUM LENGTH: 4 in. (10 cm).

NATIVE RANGE: Rocky shoreline of Lake Tanganyika.

MINIMUM AQUARIUM SIZE: 30 gal. (114 L).

GENERAL SWIMMING LEVEL: Bottom to midwater.

OVERVIEW: The Tanganyikan Lemon Cichlid is a beautiful slender fish with an engaging personality. Its entire body, including the fins, is a deep, rich yellow. They typically have a semi-circular, thin blue line under the eye.

FEEDING: Omnivore. In the wild, the Lemon Cichlid feeds carnivorously on micro-invertebrates but will accept any of the many commercial high-protein cichlid diets intended for Rift Lake predators, as well as freeze-dried and frozen foods, such as brine shrimp and bloodworms. Their diets should also include live foods, and they will also benefit from color-enhancing foods.

HABITAT: These fishes are found among caves and crevices in nature and should be provided similar shelters in the aquarium in the form of rockwork to form caves. They require hard, alkaline water, so a dolomite or coral-based gravel substrate is best.

AQUARIUM CARE/BEHAVIOR: Start with a small group and let them pair up. They can be housed with some other Lake Tanganyikan cichlids, but belligerent encounters may happen.

BREEDING: Lemon Cichlids are serially monogamous, cave-spawning fishes that often form temporary pair bonds. The female lays eggs on the ceiling of a cave and tends to the fry, while the male guards the territory in the aquarium.

AURATUS
Melanochromis auratus
Length: 4.3 in. (11 cm)

FUELLEBORNI
Labeotropheus fuelleborni
Max. Length: 6 in. (15 cm)

GOLDEN TROPHEOPS
Pseudotropheus tropheops
Length: 5.5 in. (14 cm)

KENYI
Pseudotropheus lombardoi
Length: 3.4 in. (8.7 cm)

MALAWI ZEBRA
Metriaclima zebra
Length: 4.4 in. (11.3 cm)

SOCOLOFI
Pseudotropheus socolofi
Max. Length: 3 in. (7 cm)

YELLOW LABIDO *Labidochromis caeruleus*
(Electric Yellow Cichlid, Pearl Labidochromis)

MAXIMUM LENGTH: 3 in. (8 cm).

NATIVE RANGE: Scattered localities in Lake Malawi.

MINIMUM AQUARIUM SIZE: 30 gal. (114 L).

GENERAL SWIMMING LEVEL: Everywhere.

OVERVIEW: The Yellow Labido is a glorious, slinky fish and among the least aggressive of the Lake Malawi Mbunas ("um-boo-nas" or rock dwellers). Males have a bright-yellow body color with black pigment in their fins.

FEEDING: Omnivore. Yellow Labidochromis are not fussy eaters. Provide them with a varied diet that includes good-quality flake and pelleted foods, some of which contain vegetable (*Spirulina*) matter. Bloodworms, brine shrimp and other meaty foods are also appreciated, and color-enhancing foods will maintain the intense yellow color.

HABITAT: The Yellow Labido is a rock-dwelling mbuna that requires an environment with lots rockwork and caves (piles of rocks or flowerpots) so that each male can have its own territory. They need hard, alkaline water to do best, so provide a fine-grade dolomite or coral-based gravel substrate and leave some open swimming room. They are hard on live plants, so choose artificial or unpalatable varieties like Java Fern. Good filtration and regular water changes are a must.

AQUARIUM CARE/BEHAVIOR: The Yellow Labido can be successfully maintained in a tank with other mbunas. It is best to acquire a group of one male to several females.

BREEDING: Mouthbrooding cave spawners that will breed readily.

GIANT DANIO *Devario aequipinnatus*

MAXIMUM LENGTH: 6 in. (15 cm).
NATIVE RANGE: India and Sri Lanka.
MINIMUM AQUARIUM SIZE: 30 gal. (114 L) long.
GENERAL SWIMMING LEVEL: Midwater to top.
OVERVIEW: The Giant Danio is a sleek, athletic fish with a great disposition. It brings constant swimming action to a community tank and should be kept in schools of at least 3 to 5 fish. It may be a bit too active for small, peaceful tanks and is more appropriate in a community of larger fishes.
FEEDING: Omnivore. The diet of the Giant Danio should include both meaty and vegetable-based fare. Feed a wide variety of prepared aquarium foods, including *Spirulina*-based flakes, freeze-dried and frozen foods. Treat with occasional live foods like brine shrimp and bloodworms to help enhance their coloration.
HABITAT: The Giant Danio deserves a larger aquarium of 30 or more gallons, although initially, smaller aquariums will do quite well. Long is more important than tall, as they need lots of room for their end-to-end swimming patterns. These are jumpers, so a tight-fitting top is a must. A cover of floating plants and a dark substrate will help to show off their colors.
AQUARIUM CARE/BEHAVIOR: Although the Giant Danio schools at the surface in the wild, in the aquarium it typically spends its time in the middle and upper regions, depending on where there is more open water to roam.
BREEDING: In the manner of Barbs, it scatters adhesive eggs among clumps of plants.

PEARL DANIO *Danio albolineatus*

MAXIMUM LENGTH: 2.5 in. (6.5 cm), with females larger than males.

NATIVE RANGE: Southeast Asia.

MINIMUM AQUARIUM SIZE: 10 gal. (38 L).

GENERAL SWIMMING LEVEL: Throughout the aquarium.

OVERVIEW: Danios are very busy fish and perfect for the aquarist who likes a lively aquascape with lots of movement. The Pearl Danio is a peaceful, schooling species. The natural version of the Pearl Danio is a lovely "mother-of-pearl" species, with a pinkish-blue iridescent body. There is also a gold variety, called the Yellow Danio, which is derived from aquarium-bred stock.

FEEDING: Carnivore. In the wild, their diets consist primarily of insects and insect larvae, and in the aquarium they will accept most commercial aquarium foods, including good-quality tropical flake or granular food, as well as frozen and live foods such as *Tubifex*, mosquito larvae, brine shrimp and *Daphnia*. Will benefit from regular feedings of color-enhancing foods.

HABITAT: *D. albolineatus* does best in a well-lighted aquarium planted on the sides and back, with lots of room in the center to swim. A long tank is ideal for providing the room they need to stretch their fins.

AQUARIUM CARE/BEHAVIOR: Acquire a group of at least three and house with other mild-mannered fish. These are jumpers, so a tight-fitting cover is a must.

BREEDING: During frantic chases, they scatter non-adhesive eggs that fall to the bottom. Shallow water and a marble-covered bottom will prevent the parents from eating their own spawn.

ZEBRA DANIO *Danio rerio*
(Zebra Fish)

MAXIMUM LENGTH: 2.5 in. (6 cm).
NATIVE RANGE: Eastern India, but most commercially bred.
MINIMUM AQUARIUM SIZE: 10 gal. (38 L).
GENERAL SWIMMING LEVEL: Throughout the aquarium.
OVERVIEW: The Zebra Danio has been kept by tropical fish fanciers for more than a century and still ranks as one of the best-liked and hardy beginner's species. When kept in schools, as it should be, it puts on a constant show of flashing stripes without threatening other peaceful fishes. A variety of color morphs and long-fin varieties have been commercially developed, including albino, veiltail and leopard varieties. Zebras are extensively used in scientific genome research.
FEEDING: Omnivore. Will accept most aquarium foods, including flakes, freeze-dried and frozen. Supplement their diets with *Spirulina*-based foods. Treat occasionally with live foods like brine shrimp and bloodworms.
HABITAT: The Zebra Danio prefers a well-lighted aquarium with good circulation. Include plants on the sides and back, with lots of open area in the center for swimming. Decorate with driftwood or a few rocks and a fine-grade gravel substrate.
AQUARIUM CARE/BEHAVIOR: The Zebra Danio is an active schooling species that should be kept in groups of at least three. They are jumpers—keep under a tight-fitting cover.
BREEDING: Males are torpedo shaped, while females are usually larger and more full-bodied. The Zebra Danio is an easy-to-breed egg scatterer. The first egglaying species for many beginning breeders.

FLYING FOX *Epalzeorhynchos kalopterus*

MAXIMUM LENGTH: 6.2 in. (16 cm).

NATIVE RANGE: Malayasia, Thailand, Indonesia.

MINIMUM AQUARIUM SIZE: 29 gal. (110 L).

GENERAL SWIMMING LEVEL: Bottom to midwater.

OVERVIEW: While it is often mistaken for a catfish, this fish is classified with the barbs and upon close inspection will be seen to have two pairs of barbels on the upper lip. The similar-looking Siamese Algae Eater (page 125) has only a single pair. Like the Siamese Algae Eater, it has a black horizontal stripe that extends from the snout to the fork of the tail fin, although the portion running through the tail fin is darker and thicker in this species. Unlike the Siamese Algae Eater, it will not keep the tank free of algae, although it may eat plants. It has the peculiar habit of resting on plant leaves or the substrate on its pectoral fins. It is a reasonably good community fish, but will battle with other Flying Foxes and should be kept singly.

FEEDING: Omnivore. Feed a good variety of prepared foods. *Spirulina* should be a regular part of the diet. The addition of some meaty foods is also recommended.

HABITAT: The Flying Fox prefers a densely planted aquarium that includes lots of rocks and driftwood to hide among. Provide a fine-grade gravel substrate and moderate to strong current. Regular water changes are appreciated.

AQUARIUM CARE/BEHAVIOR: Although otherwise peaceful, the Flying Fox is a solitary, territorial species that will defend its space and becomes more aggressive with age. Keep only one per tank.

BREEDING: No spawnings reported in the aquarium.

KISSING GOURAMI *Helostoma temminckii*

MAXIMUM LENGTH: 12 in. (30 cm), although aquarium specimens are smaller.

NATIVE RANGE: Thailand, Malaysia, Borneo, Java, Sumatra.

MINIMUM AQUARIUM SIZE: 55 gal. (208 L).

GENERAL SWIMMING LEVEL: Midwater to top.

OVERVIEW: This species is a curiosity, a fish with prominent fleshy lips that it uses to "kiss" plants, aquarium walls and, occasionally, its tankmates. Wild forms are gray to green, and most aquarium specimens have been selectively bred to display a pink color. Lip-to-lip kissing is a rare event and is a behavior indicative of the manner in which males fight over territories—they "press" their mouths together. This is a large gourami that will outgrow small tanks.

FEEDING: Herbivore. Will eat algae off plant leaves and aquarium glass. Accepts a wide range of vegetable-based aquarium foods, including *Spirulina* flakes, frozen and freeze-dried foods, as well as well-rinsed Romaine lettuce, parboiled zucchini or peas.

HABITAT: Prefers a well-decorated tank with ample swimming space. It is good to choose artificial plants or unpalatable live plants, such as Java fern, as this fish will eat plants.

AQUARIUM CARE/BEHAVIOR: Tolerant toward conspecifics and other fishes of similar size, and although males may occasionally become aggressive toward one another, no harm is done during these interactions. Can be housed with larger mid- to top-water swimmers, including barbs, danios and angelfish.

BREEDING: They do not build bubblenests. Eggs adhere to floating plants or leaves. No parental care and may eat the fry.

BLUE GOURAMI *Trichogaster trichopterus*
(Three-Spot Gourami)

MAXIMUM LENGTH: 6 in. (15 cm).

NATIVE RANGE: Southeast Asia.

MINIMUM AQUARIUM SIZE: 40 gal. (150 L).

GENERAL SWIMMING LEVEL: Midwater to top.

OVERVIEW: This is a peaceful, robust bubblenester that fits nicely in a peaceful community of larger species. It is usually silvery blue in color, and several color varieties are available, including the opaline and gold gouramis. The wild Three-spot form is usually a silvery fish, while the more popular Blue Gourami has been developed from specimens collected in Sumatra.

FEEDING: Omnivore. The Blue Gourami will accept just about any aquarium fare, including good-quality flakes and freeze-dried foods, frozen foods, such as *Daphnia* and brine shrimp, as well as live foods, including bloodworms and tubificid worms. Supplement with some type of vegetable-based food. Prized for their appetite for the aquarium pest, *Hydra*.

HABITAT: Prefers a densely planted aquarium with a cover of floating plants, as well as hiding places in the form of rocks and driftwood. Provide a dark substrate to best show off their colors.

AQUARIUM CARE/BEHAVIOR: Should be housed with fishes of similar size and temperament. Best kept in a group of one male to two females—only one male per tank, as they may fight. If kept with aggressive or fin-nipping species, such as barbs, will spend most of the time hiding in the corners of the aquarium.

BREEDING: Male builds bubblenest early in the day.

CROAKING GOURAMI *Trichopsis vittata*
(Talking Gourami)

MAXIMUM LENGTH: 2.75 in. (7 cm).
NATIVE RANGE: Southeast Asia, Indonesia.
MINIMUM AQUARIUM SIZE: 5 gal. (19 L).
GENERAL SWIMMING LEVEL: Midwater.
OVERVIEW: The Croaking Gourami is so named because both males and females emit croaking noises during breeding, with the males croaking more loudly during their displays of dominance. The sound is produced by air in the fish's labyrinth apparatus, the complex organ that allows bubblenesting species to breathe air at the surface.
FEEDING: The Croaking Gourami will accept a wide variety of commercial aquarium fare, including good-quality flake foods (include algae-based flakes), as well as frozen and freeze-dried bloodworms, tubificid worms and brine shrimp. Supplement with occasional live foods, such as bloodworms, to best view their natural hunting behaviors.
HABITAT: *Trichopsis vittata* prefers a well-planted aquarium, with hiding places in the form of rocks, driftwood or inverted flowerpots, as this species is fairly timid. Include a layer of floating plants. A darker substrate will make them feel more comfortable and help show off their colors.
AQUARIUM CARE/BEHAVIOR: This is a good community fish, although males are likely to scrap with each other, especially during spawning. Keep one male with two or more females.
BREEDING: The male builds a bubblenest under leaves at the surface, as illustrated in the photograph above. Male is the upper fish, with longer fins. Female has a more rounded shape.

DWARF CROAKING GOURAMI *Trichopsis pumila*
(Pygmy Gourami)

MAXIMUM LENGTH: 1.5 in. (4 cm).

NATIVE RANGE: Southeast Asia, Indonesia.

MINIMUM AQUARIUM SIZE: 2 gal. (8 L).

GENERAL SWIMMING LEVEL: Midwater.

OVERVIEW: Like the Croaking Gourami, this species makes audible clicking sounds. These fish are tiny and delicate and are ideally kept in a "nano-tank" dedicated to their needs with other small, mild-mannered species.

FEEDING: Omnivore. The natural diet of this fish consists of tiny insects and insect larvae. They will accept meaty foods in the aquarium, including flakes, freeze-dried, frozen and live foods. Occasional meals of herbivore-type foods will be taken.

HABITAT: The Dwarf Croaking Gourami prefers an aquarium well planted with broad-leaved plants, such as *Echinodorus*, as well as a cover of floating plants. Provide ample hiding places in the form of driftwood, rocks and inverted flowerpots. A dark substrate will make them feel comfortable and show off their colors.

AQUARIUM CARE/BEHAVIOR: *T. pumila* is a peaceful, small gourami that may become aggressive during spawning. Keep in groups of one male to two or more females. They should only be housed with fishes of similar temperament and size, as more assertive species will outcompete them for food. Known fin-nippers, such as Tiger Barbs or large danios, should also be avoided.

BREEDING: The male builds a bubblenest under a large leaf and tends to the eggs and fry.

DWARF GOURAMI *Colisa lalia*

MAXIMUM LENGTH: 3 in. (8 cm).

NATIVE RANGE: India, Pakistan, Bangladesh.

MINIMUM AQUARIUM SIZE: 5 gal. (19 L).

GENERAL SWIMMING LEVEL: Midwater.

OVERVIEW: This is a great beginner's fish, provided it is kept with other small, peaceful species. The males are often spectacularly hued, with iridescent bars and orange-red feelers. A number of captive-bred color forms are commonly available.

FEEDING: Omnivore. The Dwarf Gourami is not difficult to feed in the aquarium. It will accept a wide variety of aquarium fare, including good-quality flake, freeze-dried and tableted meaty and vegetable foods. Supplement with periodic feedings of live foods, such as bloodworms.

HABITAT: The Dwarf Gourami prefers a heavily planted tank with a cover of floating plants. A darker substrate will help show off the gourami's colors. Good filtration and regular water changes are a must, as this gourami may be susceptible to disease.

AQUARIUM CARE/BEHAVIOR: Keep in pairs or in small groups of at least three (i.e., one male to two females), as this timid fish is apt to hide when kept alone. It is an ideal community fish that may become somewhat aggressive during courtship. Their delicate trailing pelvic fins are a temptation to some other fishes, so avoid keeping them with known fin nippers.

BREEDING: The Dwarf Gourami will incorporate bits of floating plants into its bubblenest. After spawning, the male guards the nest, eggs and young fry.

HONEY GOURAMI *Trichogaster chuna*

MAXIMUM LENGTH: 2.75 in. (7 cm).
NATIVE RANGE: India, Bangladesh.
MINIMUM AQUARIUM SIZE: 5 gal. (19 L).
GENERAL SWIMMING LEVEL: Midwater to top.
OVERVIEW: When in breeding condition, the males of this species are nothing short of stunning, with a brick-red to yellow dorsal fin, an orangish-red body and a bluish-black band that extends from the head to the front part of the anal fin. Out of breeding condition, they are less striking, but are very peaceful fish for a quiet community tank.
FEEDING: Omnivore. The Honey Gourami is not finicky, and it will accept a wide variety of aquarium fare, including good-quality flake, freeze-dried and tableted vegetable foods containing *Spirulina*. Supplement with periodic feedings of live foods, such as bloodworms and *Tubifex* worms.
HABITAT: The Honey Gourami prefers a tank that is densely planted on the back and sides, with a cover of floating plants. A dark gravel substrate will help to show off its colors.
AQUARIUM CARE/BEHAVIOR: The Honey Gourami is generally a peaceful species that can be kept with species of similar temperament. During breeding, the males may become quite territorial and will chase and court females. Keep in pairs, or small groups of at least one male to two females.
BREEDING: Male constructs a loose bubblenest. He will entice the female to join him under the nest, where she will lay eggs for him to fertilize and care for until the fry are free swimming.

MOONLIGHT GOURAMI *Trichogaster microlepis*

MAXIMUM LENGTH: 6 in. (15 cm).
NATIVE RANGE: Thailand, Cambodia.
MINIMUM AQUARIUM SIZE: 40 gal. (152 L).
GENERAL SWIMMING LEVEL: Midwater to top.
OVERVIEW: The Moonlight Gourami is a metallic beauty that attains a respectable size, but is bit shy and sensitive, so it should only be kept with the most docile of tankmates. Their bodies are easily damaged with rough handling and care must be taken when moving this fish.
FEEDING: Omnivore. The Moonlight Gourami is not difficult to feed and will accept a wide variety of flake, frozen, freeze-dried and live foods. This is a timid species, so take care to ensure that the Moonlight Gourami is actually receiving the food.
HABITAT: *Trichogaster microlepis* prefers an aquarium densely planted with sturdy plants, such as giant *Vallisneria* and Java fern. Fine-leaved plants will be pecked to death, and the rotting leaves will cause water-quality deterioration. Provide cover in the form of driftwood and aquarium ornaments for this shy species to get out of the limelight when necessary. Good filtration and regular water changes are a must.
AQUARIUM CARE/BEHAVIOR: The Moonlight Gourami should be kept with fishes of similar size and meek temperament. Obtain a small group—one male to two females—to make them feel more comfortable.
BREEDING: Builds bubblenests that include bits of plants. Lowered water levels and tank covers are necessary for breeding success.

PEARL GOURAMI *Trichogaster leerii*
(Mosaic Gourami, Lace Gourami)

MAXIMUM LENGTH: 4 in. (12 cm).

NATIVE RANGE: Southeast Asia and Indonesia.

MINIMUM AQUARIUM SIZE: 20 gal. (76 L).

GENERAL SWIMMING LEVEL: Midwater to top.

OVERVIEW: The Pearl Gourami is among the loveliest of all the aquarium fishes, sedate and elegant. It is a curious fish that utilizes its "feelers," modified pelvic fins, to investigate its surroundings. This is the hardiest of all gouramis and long lived—up to eight years.

FEEDING: Omnivore. The Pearl Gourami is relatively easy to feed and will accept a variety of foods, including tropical flakes, freeze-dried and frozen foods. Green foods are important in the Pearl's diet, and this fish is well-known to consume unsightly filamentous algae. Live foods, such as black worms, brine shrimp and glass worms, are also relished.

HABITAT: *T. leerii* prefers a tank that is well planted and with dark and bright areas to suit the fish's moods. Generally, this fish will stay in the open and occupy the center of the tank.

AQUARIUM CARE/BEHAVIOR: Keep one male with one or two females. Eats hydra. Peaceful species that should not be combined with aggressive fishes, such as cichlids, as it may hide in the corners and refuse to eat. Keep only with mild-mannered bottom or mid-water species. Take care when moving this fish, as it is vulnerable to fungus when the slime coat is damaged.

BREEDING: Builds a large bubblenest among floating plants. Males tend the eggs and fry.

THICK-LIPPED GOURAMI *Colisa labiosus*

MAXIMUM LENGTH: 3.5 in. (9 cm).

NATIVE RANGE: Burma, Northern India.

MINIMUM AQUARIUM SIZE: 10 gal. (38 L).

GENERAL SWIMMING LEVEL: Midwater to top.

OVERVIEW: The Thick-Lipped Gourami is among the larger of the dwarf gouramis. This languid fish will investigate its surroundings with its delicate feelers. This is a peaceful and good community citizen that should be kept with similar mild-mannered fishes.

FEEDING: Another gourami that is not particularly fussy when it comes to feeding, the Thick-Lipped Gourami will accept a wide variety of aquarium foods, including good-quality flake, freeze-dried and tableted vegetable foods. Supplement with periodic feedings of live foods, such as bloodworms and tubificid worms.

HABITAT: A well-planted tank with a cover of floating plants and a dark substrate is the ideal environment for *Colisa labiosus*. This species is susceptible to disease and will not tolerate poor water conditions, so good filtration and regular water changes are a must.

AQUARIUM CARE/BEHAVIOR: Tends to be shy in the presence of boisterous tankmates. They make a fine choice for a small species tank. Keep one male to one or two females.

BREEDING: Bubblenest builder. The male will guard the nest and newly hatched fry, and like other bubblenest-building anabantids provides excellent attention to the glass-like wrigglers for the few days until they become mature enough to escape from the bubblenest permanently. Even after the brood is independent of the father's attention, they school together for some time.

GUPPY *Poecilia reticulata*
(Millions Fish) (Male, left. Gravid female, right.)

MAXIMUM LENGTH: Male 1.5 in. (3.5 cm), female 2 in. (5 cm).

NATIVE RANGE: Central and northern South America, also commercially bred in Asia, as well as local breeders.

MINIMUM AQUARIUM SIZE: 20 gal. (76 L) long.

GENERAL SWIMMING LEVEL: Midwater to top.

OVERVIEW: The Guppy is easy to keep, beautiful and inexpensive, and, if you have a male and female, odds are close to 100 percent that you'll get baby guppies. Fancy guppies appear in a staggering array of colors and finnages thanks to decades of selective breeding. Endler's Livebearer is a wild-type guppy cousin.

FEEDING: Omnivore. Guppies are not picky eaters and will accept just about anything offered to them. Feed several times per day.

HABITAT: The Guppy prefers a well-lighted tank densely planted on the sides and back. Long tanks are best, as they need lots of room to swim. Give them a little water movement with an airstone or small powerhead pump to better mimic their natural stream habitats.

AQUARIUM CARE/BEHAVIOR: Guppies are schooling fish and best kept in groups of one male to several females. Combine with other active schooling species or keep in a species tank. Known fin nippers like the Tiger Barb, may nip at their fins and should be avoided.

BREEDING: Guppies are livebearers that give birth to fully formed babies. Parents will eat their young, and pregnant females should be moved to breeding traps or tanks with Java moss or other fine-leaved plants such as *Cabomba*. One mating allows a female to produce multiple broods of young over a period of months.

GUPPY
Poecilia reticulata
Length: 2 in. (5 cm)

GUPPY
Poecilia reticulata
Length: 2 in. (5 cm)

GUPPY
Poecilia reticulata
Length: 2 in. (5 cm)

GUPPY
Poecilia reticulata
Length: 2 in. (5 cm)

GUPPY
Poecilia reticulata
Length: 2 in. (5 cm)

ENDLER'S LIVEBEARER
Poecilia sp.
Length: 2 in. (5 cm)

MARBLED HATCHETFISH *Carnegiella strigata*

MAXIMUM LENGTH: 1.4 in. (3.5 cm).

NATIVE RANGE: South America, Amazon River, Caqueta River.

MINIMUM AQUARIUM SIZE: 20 gal. (76 L) long.

GENERAL SWIMMING LEVEL: Top.

OVERVIEW: The smaller of the two commonly available hatchet-fishes, this is an eyecatching little surface dweller that fits nicely into more peaceful community settings. In the wild it is found in schools and it puts on a wonderful show when kept in groups of five or more. It will do best in a long tank with plenty of swimming room and if other surface-dwelling species are absent.

FEEDING: Carnivore. It feeds only at or near the surface and must be fed accordingly. Offer high-protein floating prepared foods as well as a diet of small frozen or live foods, such as brine shrimp and *Daphnia*. Hatchetfishes will starve if not fed properly.

HABITAT: In the wild, this fish is found in fast-moving streams with lots of vegetation, a biotope that should be closely mimicked in the aquarium. Include floating plants, such as duckweed and water sprite, but make sure to leave plenty of open areas at the surface.

AQUARIUM CARE/BEHAVIOR: Hatchetfishes can literally fly out of the water (see Silver Hatchetfish) and they must be housed in covered aquariums. It does not compete well with big, boisterous tankmates and will do best with peaceful community fishes that tend to stay in the lower levels of the tank.

BREEDING: Eggs are scattered to drop among plants or gravel and hatch within 36 hours. Females have larger abdomens than males.

SILVER HATCHETFISH *Gasteropelecus sternicla*
(Common Hatchetfish)

MAXIMUM LENGTH: 2.5 in. (6.5 cm).

NATIVE RANGE: Brazil, Guyana, Surinam.

MINIMUM AQUARIUM SIZE: 20 gal. (76 L) long.

GENERAL SWIMMING LEVEL: Top.

OVERVIEW: The Common Hatchetfish has a fascinating anatomy with an upturned mouth designed for capturing low-flying insects or insect larvae at the surface of the water. Modified pectoral fins allow the fish to become briefly airborne, appearing to "fly" across the surface of the water.

FEEDING: Carnivore. It feeds only at or near the surface and must be fed accordingly. Offer high-protein floating prepared foods as well as a diet of small frozen or live foods, such as brine shrimp and *Daphnia*. Hatchetfishes will starve if not fed properly.

HABITAT: In the wild, this fish is found in fast-moving streams with lots of vegetation, a biotope that should be closely mimicked in the aquarium. Include floating plants, such as duckweed and water sprite, but make sure to leave plenty of open areas at the surface.

AQUARIUM CARE/BEHAVIOR: A peaceful surface dweller, this is a schooling species that does best when kept in groups of at least three. It is somewhat skittish, so keep it with peaceful community fishes that occupy lower tank levels. Keep their tank tightly covered, with no gaps for them to sail through.

BREEDING: Egg scatterer among plants. Females are typically larger than males. Difficult to spawn and rear the young.

BENGAL LOACH *Botia dario*
(Queen Loach, Geto Loach)

MAXIMUM LENGTH: 6 in. (15 cm).
NATIVE RANGE: India, Bangladesh, Bhutan.
MINIMUM AQUARIUM SIZE: 55 gal. (208 L).
GENERAL SWIMMING LEVEL: Bottom.

OVERVIEW: This is one of the truly delightful loaches and a favorite fish of all who have kept it. When acquired in groups of at least three, the Bengal Loach will provide the aquarist hours of entertainment, swimming in the characteristic loach "dance," as it is commonly referred to, in which a group swims up and down in the water in figure-eight patterns.

FEEDING: Omnivore. These are bottom feeders that spend much of their time foraging for bits of food in the substrate. They will accept a wide variety of commercial flake foods and sinking pellets, as well as live or frozen bloodworms or brine shrimp.

HABITAT: Because they are bottom dwellers that burrow in the substrate, the Bengal Loach tank should consist of fine-grained, round-edged gravel. Include numerous hiding places in the form of driftwood or inverted flowerpots to make them feel secure enough to exhibit their natural behaviors.

AQUARIUM CARE/BEHAVIOR: Bengal Loaches are often seen "play fighting" over bits of food when kept in groups of three or more in a community setting, but don't be alarmed—it's just an act and no one gets hurt. These are scaleless fishes that are particularly susceptible to ich. Use only medications designated for scaleless fishes.

BREEDING: Not reported in the aquarium.

CLOWN LOACH *Chromobotia macracanthus*

MAXIMUM LENGTH: 12 in. (30 cm).

NATIVE RANGE: Malaysia and parts of Indonesia.

MINIMUM AQUARIUM SIZE: 55 gal. (208 L).

GENERAL SWIMMING LEVEL: Bottom to midwater.

OVERVIEW: The best known of the loaches, the Clown Loach is a beautiful fish that is relatively long lived. It can start out in a 30-gallon (114 L) tank, but can grow large and will eventually need more spacious quarters. They are best kept in groups of at least three to enjoy their comical behaviors.

FEEDING: Omnivore. Will accept a wide variety of live or frozen foods, including brine shrimp, bloodworms and mosquito larvae. Supplement with commercial algae or carnivore wafers, as well as herbivore fare and color-enhancing flakes.

HABITAT: Prefers an aquarium with subdued lighting and efficient filtration, as they are susceptible to poor water quality. Frequent partial water changes are a must. Provide fine-grade or smooth gravel substrate and plants should be artificial or potted and buried in the substrate.

AQUARIUM CARE/BEHAVIOR: Although the Clown Loach is nocturnal, this species is seen out in the open during the day, mostly early in the morning when the lights are turned on and at dusk. It has the peculiar habit of "playing dead" on the bottom of the aquarium. Don't be fooled—they are just resting. They also make "clicking" sounds like many other loaches. As scaleless fishes, they are susceptible to ich and should always be quarantined when first acquired.

BREEDING: There are no reports of aquarium breeding to date.

DWARF LOACH *Yasuhikotakia sidthimunki*
(Dwarf Chain Loach, Dwarf Botia, Chipmunk Botia)

MAXIMUM LENGTH: 2.3 in. (6 cm).

NATIVE RANGE: Cambodia, Laos, Thailand.

MINIMUM AQUARIUM SIZE: 20 gal. (76 L).

GENERAL SWIMMING LEVEL: Bottom.

OVERVIEW: The smallest member of the loach group, the Dwarf Loach also has a repertoire of unique behaviors and makes a droll, entertaining resident of a peaceful community aquarium. Although this is an endangered species in its native Thailand, large numbers of commercially bred individuals are now available.

FEEDING: Easy to feed, the Dwarf Loach will accept most small foods offered, including sinking catfish pellets, micropellets, flakes, algae wafers and small-size frozen foods, such as *Daphnia*, *Cyclops* and brine shrimp.

HABITAT: An aquarium for the Dwarf Loach should include fine-grade or rounded gravel substrate in order to protect the fish's delicate sensory barbels. Include driftwood, rocky caves and aquatic plants as hiding places. Excellent filtration is a must.

AQUARIUM CARE/BEHAVIOR: Like all loaches, the Dwarf Loach should be kept in groups of at least three to make them comfortable enough to exhibit their wide array of behaviors. Unlike many of the others in their family that wait until after dark to become active, these little loaches like to school in the mid-water environs of their aquariums during the day.

BREEDING: None, although some aquarists have reported pre-spawning activity in their fishes.

KUHLI LOACH *Pangio kuhlii*
(Coolie Loach. Prickly Eye)

MAXIMUM LENGTH: 4 in. (10 cm).

NATIVE RANGE: Southern Thailand, parts of Malaysia and Indonesia.

MINIMUM AQUARIUM SIZE: 10 gal. (38 L).

GENERAL SWIMMING LEVEL: Bottom.

OVERVIEW: With a life-span of 10+ years, the eel-shaped Kuhli Loach makes an interesting, hardy addition to a peaceful community aquarium. Be careful—it possesses sharp cheek spines.

FEEDING: Omnivore. It will accept a wide variety of commercial foods, including good-quality flakes, sinking pellets and frozen foods, such as bloodworms, mysid shrimp and brine shrimp. Feed first thing in the morning and just after the lights go out at night.

HABITAT: Kuhli Loaches love planted aquariums with plenty of cover. Because they are sensitive to poor water quality, place in well-established aquariums only. Provide lots of hiding places and, because they spend their time burrowing in the sand in search of food, include a fine-grade or rounded gravel substrate.

AQUARIUM CARE/BEHAVIOR: Once acclimated, Kuhli Loaches are relatively undemanding and should be kept in groups of at least three to better enjoy their full range of antics. While it is possible to keep just one, this is a stressful existence for such a gregarious species and you may not even realize you have one, as it will remain hidden. Kept in groups, they will become quite active, exhibiting all the "loachy" behaviors aquarists have come to know and love.

BREEDING: May occasionally spawn in the aquarium, but few reports have been made to date.

REDTAIL BOTIA *Yasuhikotakia modesta*
(Blue Botia, Red-Finned Loach)

MAXIMUM LENGTH: 8 in. (20 cm).

NATIVE RANGE: Southeast Asia.

MINIMUM AQUARIUM SIZE: 40 gal. (152 L).

GENERAL SWIMMING LEVEL: Bottom.

OVERVIEW: This is one of the more heavy-bodied loaches, a substantial and lovely fish with a bluish gray body. Its fins come in a variety of colors, including red, orange and yellow.

FEEDING: Redtail Botia are greedy eaters that will accept a wide variety of good-quality flake foods, sinking pellets, algae wafers and frozen foods, such as bloodworms and mysid shrimp.

HABITAT: Although they will become quite large, initially they can be kept in a smaller, 20-gal. (76 L) aquarium with excellent filtration. They prefer subdued lighting and are active diggers that will require a fine-grade or smooth gravel substrate in which to "grub." Somewhat rowdy, so provide plenty of hiding places for other fish to escape them.

AQUARIUM CARE/BEHAVIOR: Because of their rowdy temperaments, these fishes should be kept with similar fish, such as barbs. To best see their playful antics, keep a group of at least three. Like the Clown and other loaches, these fishes also have a distinct hierarchy, with a definite "boss fish." They are highly territorial and may make "clicking" sounds during feeding and periods of in-fighting. They possess cheek spines that may become entangled in nets.

BREEDING: Not reported in the aquarium.

MOLLY *Poecilia sphenops*
(Black Molly, Short-finned Molly)

MAXIMUM LENGTH: 2.3 in. (6 cm).
NATIVE RANGE: Central America.
MINIMUM AQUARIUM SIZE: 20 long or 30 gal. (76-114 L).
GENERAL SWIMMING LEVEL: Midwater to top.
OVERVIEW: The Molly is a hardy, stocky-bodied (spheno = "wedge shaped") species that, unlike its sailfin counterpart, lacks the elaborate dorsal fin. Because they are often found in mangrove swamps, estuaries and many other "salty" environs, many saltwater hobbyists use molly fry as food for their fishes, because of the molly's ability to do well in saltwater tanks. Breeders have developed many color strains, including marbled, orange and blue forms. (See the specimens on page 117, illustrating marbling and two color variations.)
FEEDING: Omnivore. It is important that their diets not only include meaty prepared foods, but also lots of plant matter, such as algae wafers and *Spirulina*-based flake foods.
HABITAT: Mollies will acclimate to the typical community tank water parameters, but adding some aquarium or sea salt to the water (1-2 level teaspoons per gallon) will ensure a healthier slime coat, and for most other fishes this will not be a problem.
AQUARIUM CARE/BEHAVIOR: Acquire one male to several females to reduce the male's harrassing any single female. Keep with other peaceful community tank fishes.
BREEDING: Mollies are livebearers that tend to be less prolific than their counterparts.

SAILFIN MOLLY *Poecilia velifera*
(Platinum Sailfin Molly pair, above. Female, left; male right.)

MAXIMUM LENGTH: 4.75 in. (12 cm).

NATIVE RANGE: Cental America, southeastern Mexico.

MINIMUM AQUARIUM SIZE: 40 gal. (152 L).

GENERAL SWIMMING LEVEL: Midwater to top.

OVERVIEW: The Sailfin Molly is larger and more robust than its short-finned relatives. Although the natural color form is quite lovely, with a nice greenish hue, this species has been commercially produced in a number of other color forms, including black, marbled and albino. Like the Black Molly, this fish is found in a number of habitats, ranging from freshwater to brackish and even saltwater. Another sailfin variety, the large Mexican Sailfin Molly (*P. latipinna*) is also available.

FEEDING: Omnivore. Provide a herbivore rations, including *Spirulina*-based flakes, algae wafers. Also offer meaty foods, such as blood-worms, dried mosquito larvae and brine shrimp.

HABITAT: The tank should be well-lit and well-planted on the sides and back with plants that can withstand a small amount of salt (Java fern, Java moss). Sailfins benefit from the addition of some salt, which will not harm most other community fishes. Must have lots of open swimming room or the male's sailfin will not develop fully.

AQUARIUM CARE/BEHAVIOR: The Sailfin Molly is a peaceful fish that will do well when kept in a group of one male to several females in a community setting with other, slightly larger, peaceful fishes.

BREEDING: The Sailfin Mollies are livebearers that are somewhat more demanding to breed in the aquarium than other livebearers. Females that are not handled properly will drop premature babies.

TANGERINE SAILFIN MOLLY
Poecilia velifera
Length: 4.75 in. (12 cm)

BLACK SAILFIN MOLLY
Poecilia velifera
Length: 4.75 in. (12 cm)

GREEN SAILFIN MOLLY
Poecilia velifera
Length: 4.75 in. (12 cm)

GREEN SAILFIN MOLLY
Poecilia velifera
Length: 4.75 in. (12 cm)

BLACK MOLLY
Poecilia sphenops
Length: 2.3 in. (6 cm)

MEXICAN SAILFIN MOLLY
Poecilia latipinna
Length: 7 in. (17.8 cm)

PLATY *Xiphophorus maculatus*
(Southern Platy Fish)

MAXIMUM LENGTH: Females 2.5 in. (6.5 cm), males smaller.

NATIVE RANGE: Mexico to Belize. Practically all stock sold today is commercially produced on fish farms.

MINIMUM AQUARIUM SIZE: 10 gal. (19 L).

GENERAL SWIMMING LEVEL: Midwater to top.

OVERVIEW: Platies are hardy fishes tolerant of a wide range of water conditions, which, along with their vibrant coloration, makes them ideal for beginners. They lack the extended tail fin or "sword" of their close relative, the Swordtail. Popular variations include the red, sunset, "wagtail" and "tuxedo" platies.

FEEDING: Omnivore. Platies eat all kinds of aquarium foods, from good-quality flakes and tableted foods, to frozen or live foods, such as bloodworms and mysid shrimp. They also require vegetable matter, so include *Spirulina*-based foods, as well as parboiled veggies.

HABITAT: Platies will appreciate a tank with live plants on the sides and back, as they may pick at them to supplement their diets. Provide good lighting and lots of open area in the center for swimming. They don't do well with lots of water movement, so less powerful filtration will better suit them.

AQUARIUM CARE/BEHAVIOR: Platies are mild-mannered fish that can be housed with a wide range of other peaceful community fishes. Acquire one male to several females.

BREEDING: Platies are livebearers and extremely easy to breed. If the parents are well fed they are less likely to cannibalize the young.

RAINBOW SHARK *Epalzeorhynchos frenatum*
(Ruby Shark, Rainbow Shark Minnow)

MAXIMUM LENGTH: 6 in. (15 cm).
NATIVE RANGE: Cambodia, Thailand.
MINIMUM AQUARIUM SIZE: 30 gal. (114 L).
GENERAL SWIMMING LEVEL: Everywhere.
OVERVIEW: Like its cousin the Flying Fox (page 96), the Rainbow Shark is an interesting fish related to the barbs and danios. It tends to be a territorial species that may be aggressive, particularly toward its own kind and should not be housed with small, passive species. An albino morph has been established. Do not purchased dyed fish sold by some stores.
FEEDING: Omnivore. The Rainbow Shark is an easy-to-feed species that will accept a wide variety of aquarium fare, including flake, freeze-dried and frozen foods. Include vegetable matter like *Spirulina*-based foods, as well. It will also graze on algae.
HABITAT: Like other members of the genus *Epalzeorhynchos*, the Rainbow Shark is a loner that prefers a densely planted aquarium decorated with rocks and driftwood, allowing the fish to avoid other tankmates during its continuous forays throughout the tank.
AQUARIUM CARE/BEHAVIOR: House as a solitary individual with other active species that occupy the midwater and upper areas of the tank like Barbs and Rainbowfish. Its aggressiveness seems to increase with age, and may be minimized with a larger aquarium and plenty of hiding places.
BREEDING: Although it has been bred in the aquarium, spawnings are rare because of its aggressive nature toward its own kind.

BANDED RAINBOWFISH *Melanotaenia trifasciata*
(Jewel Rainbowfish, Three-striped Sunfish)

MAXIMUM LENGTH: 5 in. (13 cm).
NATIVE RANGE: Northern Territory and Queensland, in Australia.
MINIMUM AQUARIUM SIZE: 30 gal. (114 L).
GENERAL SWIMMING LEVEL: Midwater to top.
OVERVIEW: Rainbowfishes are active schoolers with many admirable qualities. They are best kept in groups of two females for every male—or larger schools in bigger tanks. The Banded Rainbowfish appears in several color variants based on the river of origin. Most common is the Goyder River form replete with red fins, purplish body, and black midline band. The high arch of the back increases with age. These fish are slow to color up, requiring maturity and a mate to reach full coloration. Females are smaller than the males.
FEEDING: The Banded Rainbow is an omnivore that takes prepared, frozen and live foods with equal enthusiasm. It is an active hunter that will capture live prey the instant it hits the water.
HABITAT: The aquarium should have a layer of floating plants and be aquascaped around the perimeters, leaving plenty of open swimming room in the center. Decorate sparingly with rocks, driftwood, and a dark substrate and a planted backdrop.
AQUARIUM CARE/BEHAVIOR: Tankmates should be peaceful community types that have differing swimming habits and occupy different zones in the aquarium. These fish jump; cover the tank securely.
BREEDING: Pairs spawn in the morning and scatter the eggs, which adhere to fine-leaved plants and the roots of floating plants. Spawning mops can be used to collect eggs for hatching.

BLEHER'S RAINBOWFISH
Chilatherina bleheri
Length: 4.7 in. (12 cm)

BOESEMAN'S RAINBOWFISH
Melanotaenia boesemani
Length: 4 in. (10 cm)

GOLDIE RIVER RAINBOWFISH
Melanotaenia goldiei
Length: 3 in. (7 cm)

LAKE KUTUBU RAINBOWFISH
Melanotaenia lacustris
Length: 6 in. (15 cm)

LAKE TEBERA RAINBOWFISH
M. herbertaxelrodi
Length: 3.5 in. (9 cm)

RED RAINBOWFISH
Glossolepis incisus
Length: 6 in. (15 cm)

NEON RAINBOWFISH *Melanotaenia praecox*
(Praecox Rainbowfish, Dwarf Neon Rainbowfish)

MAXIMUM LENGTH: 2 in. (5 cm).

NATIVE RANGE: Irian Jaya, Indonesia.

MINIMUM AQUARIUM SIZE: 20 gal. (76 L).

GENERAL SWIMMING LEVEL: Midwater to top.

OVERVIEW: This is the ugly duckling of the tropical fish world: juveniles are drab and the fish only reach their beautiful coloration as they mature. This is an active schooling species that does best when kept in groups of at least three and preferably six. It is ideal if the ratio is two females to one male, but this is difficult to ensure when buying a group of young fish. Older males develop high backs.

FEEDING: *M. praecox* thrives on live foods, such as bloodworms, glassworms, brine shimp, etc., frozen, and prepared foods. Provide a varied diet.

HABITAT: Plant the tank on the sides and back and provide a cover of floating plants. A dark gravel substrate accents coloration. Allow ample open swimming space.

AQUARIUM CARE/BEHAVIOR: They're great in a peaceful community tank, but not with timid or delicate species as they can be intimidating. A well-fitted tank cover will prevent leaping losses.

BREEDING: Both sexes are vividly colored but the males do have redder fins while the fins of the females tend to range from yellow to red. A pair will scatter their eggs among the plants, several times a day as with the Banded Rainbowfish. The eggs are unusual as they can be collected and stored to hatch out later.

HARLEQUIN RASBORA *Trigonostigma heteromorpha*

MAXIMUM LENGTH: 2 in. (5 cm).
NATIVE RANGE: Thailand to Sumatra.
MINIMUM AQUARIUM SIZE: 20 gal. (76 L) long.
GENERAL SWIMMING LEVEL: Midwater to top.
OVERVIEW: One of the classic aquarium fishes, the Harlequin Rasbora is considered by many to be *the* Rasbora and an ideal choice for the peaceful community. The distinctive black "triangle on its side" is a hallmark of the species, but a second species, *T. espei*, has similar markings and is often sold as the Harlequin, although it is much slimmer.
FEEDING: Carnivore. The Harlequin Rasbora will enthusiastically accept most prepared foods, including good-quality flakes and pellets, but will need occasional feedings of frozen and live foods, such as *Daphnia* and brine shrimp, to do well in the aquarium.
Habitat: The Harlequin Rasbora prefers an environment with areas of dense vegetation and driftwood, lots of open space for swimming, a dark substrate, and a cover of floating plants to produce subdued lighting.
AQUARIUM CARE/BEHAVIOR: The Harlequin Rasbora is an active, schooling species that should be kept in groups of at least four (even more will make them feel more comfortable and provide a stunning display), with other similar-size peaceful tankmates, including many of the smaller barbs, danios or other rasboras.
BREEDING: Harlequin Rasboras are egglayers that deposit their adhesive spawns on the undersides of leaves.

SCISSORTAIL RASBORA *Rasbora trilineata*
(Three-lined Rasbora)

MAXIMUM LENGTH: 6 in. (15 cm).

NATIVE RANGE: Southeast Asia.

MINIMUM AQUARIUM SIZE: 55 gal. (209 L) long.

GENERAL SWIMMING LEVEL: Midwater to top.

OVERVIEW: While not particularly colorful, the tail fin of the silvery Scissortail Rasbora is quite eyecatching and gives rise to the fish's common name. As the fish opens and closes its tail during swimming, the black dots on the ends of the forks of the fin move up and down, giving the appearance that the tail is "slicing" through the water like a pair of scissors cutting fabric. It is larger than most other Rasboras and will outgrow small community tanks.

FEEDING: Omnivore. In nature, the Scissortail Rasbora consumes small invertebrates and will accept most commercial fare in the aquarium, including good-quality flakes, pelleted and freeze-dried foods. Treat occasionally with frozen and live foods, such as brine shrimp and bloodworms.

HABITAT: These schooling fish need room to move. The ideal is a long tank densely planted on the back with lots of open water in the center and a dark substrate to show off their striking color pattern.

AQUARIUM CARE/BEHAVIOR: Scissortail Rasboras are large, but peaceful and active schooling species perfect for a community aquarium setting. Keep in groups of at least three with other fishes of similar size and temperament. Jumper.

BREEDING: Scatters adhesive eggs among plants, but is difficult to spawn in the aquarium.

SIAMESE ALGAE EATER *Crossocheilus siamensis*

MAXIMUM LENGTH: 6 in. (15 cm).
NATIVE RANGE: Southeast Asia.
MINIMUM AQUARIUM SIZE: 30 gal. (114 L).
GENERAL SWIMMING LEVEL: Bottom.
OVERVIEW: The Siamese Algae Eater is built like a racer and is prized as the best algae eater for planted aquariums. It is distinguished from other *Crossocheilus* species in having a black longitudinal stripe on its sides. Unlike the similar-looking Flying Fox (*Epalzeorhynchos kalopterus*, page 96), the fins of this species are transparent, and it has only a single pair of barbels on the upper lip. The mouth has thick lips with many folds that form a sucking disc to rasp algae off a variety of surfaces.
FEEDING: Omnivore. *Crossocheilus siamensis* feeds on plankton and algae in the wild, and its diet in the aquarium must also include vegetable matter. Provide a variety of *Spirulina*-based foods, including flakes and wafers, as well as occasional treats of live foods like bloodworms and brine shrimp. Unlike most other algae-eating species, it will eat red and black algae, but will not harm plants.
HABITAT: Does best in a densely planted tank with driftwood or rocky aquascaping where it can graze.
AQUARIUM CARE/BEHAVIOR: The Siamese Algae Eater is a peaceful, active species best kept in groups of at least three. It can be somewhat "testy" with its own kind. Like the Flying Fox, this species also exhibits a peculiar resting position: it keeps its body "propped up" with its tail, pelvic and pectoral fins.
BREEDING: No reports of breeding in the aquarium.

SWORDTAIL *Xiphophorus helleri*
(Green Swordtail)

MAXIMUM LENGTH: Male 4 in. (10 cm), female 4.5 in. (11.5 cm).

NATIVE RANGE: Mexico to Honduras.

MINIMUM AQUARIUM SIZE: 20-30 gal. (76-114 L).

GENERAL SWIMMING LEVEL: Midwater to top.

OVERVIEW: The Swordtail takes its name from the long, saberlike extension of the male's tail fin, which is rounded in females. The original wild form is an olive-geen color. The sword itself comes in a variety of hues, from greens to yellows to oranges and reds, and many combinations thereof. They have been selectively bred to produce a large array of colors and finnages.

FEEDING: Omnivore. In the wild, plant material and insects form the major portions of their diets. In the aquarium, they will consume a wide variety of foods, such as good-quality flakes, freeze-dried , frozen or live foods like brine shrimp and mysid shrimp. To round out their diets, also offer algae-based foods, such a *Spirulina* flakes.

HABITAT: Needs a long, rather than tall, aquarium, with plants restricted to the sides and back, and plenty of room to swim in the center. Good jumpers, so a tight-fitting cover is a must.

AQUARIUM CARE/BEHAVIOR: Males are apt to bully one another, so keep only one male to several females. Sometimes they may even be a little aggressive toward other species, although they can be housed with a variety of generally peaceful, community tank fishes.

BREEDING: Classic livebearer. Will crossbreed with the closely related Platy, so it is best not to keep them in the same aquarium.

**GREEN
SWORDTAIL**
Xiphophorus helleri
Length: 4.5 in. (11.5 cm)

**EL ABRA PYGMY
SWORDTAIL** (WILD-CAUGHT)
Xiphophorus nigrensis
Length: 4.5 in. (11.5 cm)

**YELLOWFIN
SWORDTAIL**
Xiphophorus birchmanni
Length: 4.5 in. (11.5 cm)

**SWORDTAIL-PLATY
HYBRID**
Xiphophorus sp.
Length: 4.5 in. (11.5 cm)

**GREEN
SWORDTAIL**
Xiphophorus helleri
Length: 4.5 in. (11.5 cm)

**BLACK
SWORDTAIL**
Xiphophorus helleri
Length: 4.5 in. (11.5 cm)

127

BLACK PHANTOM TETRA *Hyphessobrycon megalopterus*

MAXIMUM LENGTH: 1.8 in. (4.5 cm).

NATIVE RANGE: Streams in Brazil.

MINIMUM AQUARIUM SIZE: 5 gal. (19 L).

GENERAL SWIMMING LEVEL: Midwater.

OVERVIEW: This is a lovely tetra that will provide a stunning contrast to more colorful tetras like the Cardinal Tetra. The fins of the males are black. Long-finned forms are available.

FEEDING: Carnivore. Feeds on worms, small insects and crustaceans in the wild, and is relatively easy to satisfy in the aquarium. Will accept herbivore and color-enhancing flakes.

HABITAT: The Black Phantom Tetra is found in shaded areas of rivers and lakes with dense vegetation, and will appreciate a similar environment in the aquarium. Include dense plantings of live or artificial plants on the sides and back of the aquarium, and a layer of floating plants at the surface to create the subdued lighting that will best show off their colors. Dark-colored substrate, as well as pieces of driftwood and decorations will complete the decor. Use a long aquarium to maximize swimming space. Good filtration and weekly water changes are a must for this species.

AQUARIUM CARE/BEHAVIOR: *H. megalopterus* is a peaceful, schooling species that should be kept in groups of at least three to ensure they are secure enough to exhibit their natural behaviors. Although males tend to claim small territories and will quarrel with other males, these interactions generally cause no damage.

BREEDING: Scatters eggs among plants and are easy to breed, but may become aggressive during spawning.

BLACK TETRA *Gymnocorymbus ternetzi*
(Black Widow, Skirt Tetra, White Skirt Tetra)

MAXIMUM LENGTH: 2.3 in. (6 cm).

NATIVE RANGE: Argentina, Brazil and Bolivia.

MINIMUM AQUARIUM SIZE: 5 gal. (19 L).

GENERAL SWIMMING LEVEL: Midwater.

OVERVIEW: The Black Tetra is a popular aquarium fish, highly recommended to beginners. It is commonly referred to as a Skirt Tetra, and a number of long-finned and color varieties have also been commercially produced. Avoid "painted" (dyed) fishes offered in some stores.

FEEDING: Omnivore. Not particularly finicky, it will accept just about any food in the aquarium. Provide a variety of commercial fare, including high-quality flakes, or freeze-dried or frozen foods like brine shrimp or blackworms. Supplement with vegetable-based foods, such as those that contain *Spirulina*.

HABITAT: Subdued lighting and a dark-colored gravel substrate is preferred. A long tank is best to provide them with ample room to swim in. Floating plants will help subdue the light from above. Keep the flow rate of the filter baffled to provide gentle water movement.

AQUARIUM CARE/BEHAVIOR: The Black Tetra is a peaceful, schooling species that should be kept in groups of at least three. Adults tend to be fin-nippers, so avoid tankmates with long, flowing fins.

BREEDING: This is one of the easiest of the egg scatterers to breed in the aquarium. A typical tetra breeding setup has fine-leaved plants or artificial spawning "mops" to receive the adhesive eggs and a peat moss covered bottom to create the water conditions many species prefer.

TETRA – CHARACIN • PEACEFUL

BLEEDING HEART TETRA *Hyphessobrycon erythrostigma*

MAXIMUM LENGTH: 2.75 in. (7 cm).

NATIVE RANGE: Upper Amazon River Basin, Brazil, Colombia, Peru.

MINIMUM AQUARIUM SIZE: 10 gal. (38 L).

GENERAL SWIMMING LEVEL: Midwater.

OVERVIEW: One of the best-liked tetras in the hobby, the Bleeding Heart is well-known for the bright-red, heart-shaped spot just behind the gill cover. It is a hardy species that is easy to care for in the aquarium and a reliable schooling fish for beginners. A number of similar species may be sold under the same common name.

FEEDING: Omnivore. A relatively undemanding species, the Bleeding Heart Tetra will eat just about any of the commonly available prepared foods. Provide a wide variety of commercial meaty fare, including good-quality flakes, frozen or freeze-dried foods. Supplement its diet with small live foods, such as bloodworms and brine shrimp and herbivore foods that contain *Spirulina*.

HABITAT: The Bleeding Heart Tetra prefers a shadowy tank, with clumps of larger plants on the sides and back, and smaller varieties in front, leaving lots of open area in the center for the fish to swim. Include a dark gravel substrate and decorate with driftwood.

AQUARIUM CARE/BEHAVIOR: A schooling species best kept in groups of at least three and only with mild-mannered community fishes. It is sensitive to poor water conditions, so regular water changes are a must.

BREEDING: Scatters adhesive eggs but is not easy to spawn. Males have extended dorsal and anal fins, and brighter colors.

BLOODFIN TETRA *Aphyocharax anisitsi*

MAXIMUM LENGTH: 2 in. (5.5 cm).

NATIVE RANGE: Rio Parana, Argentina.

MINIMUM AQUARIUM SIZE: 10 gal. (38 L) long.

GENERAL SWIMMING LEVEL: Typically midwater, but also top.

OVERVIEW: The Bloodfin Tetra is great schooling fish and a relatively long lived tetra—up to 10 years. Males have a small hook on the anal fin and a more slender body. There are a number of similar species that may be sold under the same common name.

FEEDING: Omnivore. The Bloodfin Tetra is not particularly finicky and will accept a varied diet of all types of commercial meaty fare, including flakes, pellets, freeze-dried, frozen and live foods.

HABITAT: *Aphyocharax anisitsi* prefers a tank well planted on the sides and back, leaving lots of open space in the center for swimming. Provide a cover of floating plants to diffuse the lighting, and a dark substrate to best show off their colors. Decorate with driftwood and rocks.

AQUARIUM CARE/BEHAVIOR: Bloodfin Tetras are extremely active schooling fishes that should be kept in groups of at least four or five. They mix well with most other community tank residents, including barbs and other tetras.

BREEDING: Bloodfins are egg scatterers and sexually dimorphic, with the males slighty more brilliant in coloration. Breeders report that this fish may leap out of the aquarium at the moment of spawning, letting the eggs fall back into the water. The non-adhesive eggs will drop to the bottom.

CARDINAL TETRA *Paracheirodon axelrodi*

MAXIMUM LENGTH: 1.5 in. (4 cm)
NATIVE RANGE: Brazil, Colombia, Venezuela.
MINIMUM AQUARIUM SIZE: 10 gal. (38 L) long.
GENERAL SWIMMING LEVEL: Midwater.
OVERVIEW: Once known as The Rich Man's Neon Tetra, the Cardinal Tetra is now a popular schooling aquarium fish commonly imported from the Amazon basin. In recent years, some hobbyists report difficulties acclimating new specimens, which may arrive from the wild malnourished and in less than ideal condition.
FEEDING: Omnivore. *Paracheirodon axelrodi* eats absolutely anything in the aquarium—flakes, pellets, freeze-dried and frozen foods, including brine shrimp, black worms and *Daphnia*. The latter foods can be used to recondition new Cardinals showing any signs of malnourishment.
HABITAT: The Cardinal Tetra is somewhat sensitive to water conditions, requiring warm, soft and acidic water to prosper. Their tanks should be well planted on the sides and back, with a layer of floating plants to diffuse the light, and plenty of room to swim in the center. A dark-colored background and substrate will help to show of the fish's colors. Decorate with driftwood and rocks.
AQUARIUM CARE/BEHAVIOR: Cardinal Tetras are small schooling fishes that should be kept in groups of six or more with other peaceful community tank residents of similar size. Do not trust them with larger fishes, such as Angelfish, that will chase and eat them.
BREEDING: Breeding in the aquarium is difficult, and most aquarium specimens are wild caught.

CONGO TETRA *Phenacogrammus interruptus*

MAXIMUM LENGTH: Males 3 in. (8 cm), females slightly smaller.

NATIVE RANGE: Congo River Basin, Africa; also commercially bred.

MINIMUM AQUARIUM SIZE: 30 gal. (114 L).

GENERAL SWIMMING LEVEL: Midwater to top.

OVERVIEW: Here is a classy species that literally sparkles. It is a popular aquarium fish that is also quite hardy. To truly appreciate the Congo Tetra's appearance, place the aquarium in an area where there is some natural light. Full-spectrum aquarium lights will also help.

FEEDING: Omnivore. In the wild, they feed mostly on insects but will accept most aquarium foods, including good-quality flakes that contain color enhancers (carotene) and vegetable matter (*Spirulina*), as well as meaty frozen and live foods like bloodworms, *Daphnia* and brine shrimp.

HABITAT: Although the Congo Tetra can be kept in smaller aquariums, these are active swimmers that are always on the go and will do best in long rather than tall tanks to provide them with lots of room. Plant along the sides and back, and provide a dark substrate and background, which will go a long way toward showcasing their colors. They are somewhat skittish, so provide a cover of floating plants to diffuse the lighting. Regular water changes are a must.

AQUARIUM CARE/BEHAVIOR: The Congo Tetra is an active, schooling species that should be kept in groups of at least three (the more, the better). They are extremely peaceful and can be mixed with most mild-mannered community fishes. Avoid fin nippers like Tiger Barbs or Redeye Tetras, as these may bite the flowing fins of the males.

BREEDING: This egg-scatterer has typical tetra spawning demands.

DIAMOND TETRA *Moenkhausia pittieri*
(Pittier's Tetra)

MAXIMUM LENGTH: Males to 2.3 in. (6 cm), females smaller.
NATIVE RANGE: Venezuela.
MINIMUM AQUARIUM SIZE: 20 gal. (76 L) long.
GENERAL SWIMMING LEVEL: Midwater.
OVERVIEW: The Diamond Tetra is a wonderful aquarium fish that only attains its most spectacular coloration as an adult. Unfortunately, juveniles offered for sale are somewhat drab and are passed over by many hobbyists. If you can, acquire a group of juveniles and watch them transform into glittery adults with bodies awash in specks of purples, greens and blues.
FEEDING: Omnivore. They will accept any of the standard aquarium fare, including good-quality flakes, frozen or freeze-dried foods like brine shrimp and bloodworms. Supplement with small live foods, such as *Daphnia*. As with most tetras, regular feedings of color-enhancing foods will help in maintaining their bright colors.
HABITAT: This is a typical tetra that loves room to exercise its swimming abilities. Does best in a long aquarium with plants restricted to the sides and back and open water in the center. Use a dark background and substrate to show off their colors. They prefer soft, acidic water.
AQUARIUM CARE/BEHAVIOR: This is a midwater schooling species that should be kept in groups of at least three with other mild-mannered community fishes. Do not combine with fin nippers. Males may display toward one another, but no harm is done.
BREEDING: Diamond Tetras are easy-to-breed egg scatterers

EMPEROR TETRA *Nematobrycon palmeri*
(Rainbow Tetra)

MAXIMUM LENGTH: 2 in. (5 cm).

NATIVE RANGE: West Coast of Colombia.

MINIMUM AQUARIUM SIZE: 20 gal. (76 L) long.

GENERAL SWIMMING LEVEL: Midwater and lower third of tank.

OVERVIEW: The Emperor Tetra is a sleek, handsome fish and a favorite of tetra enthusiasts. In the male, there is an extended black ray that runs horizontally to the end of a tail that resembles a three-pronged fork or trident. Newly imported fish in less-than-top condition may require careful feeding and conditioning time in a quarantine tank to restore their strength.

FEEDING: Omnivore. *Nematobrycon palmeri* will readily accept flake, freeze-dried and frozen meaty foods. Live foods, such as *Daphnia* and brine shrimp, are especially relished. Herbivore flakes containing *Spirulina* and color-enhancing rations should be offered regularly.

HABITAT: Emperor Tetras prefer dense vegetation and subdued lighting. A dark substrate and background will go a long way toward making them feel at home. They will thrive in even moderately hard water as long there are regular water changes. Provide them lots of swimming room to stretch their fins.

AQUARIUM CARE/BEHAVIOR: Although somewhat territorial, the Emperor Tetra is a relatively hardy, peaceful species that should not be combined with more active species and makes a good community tank resident. Keep only one male with two or more females. Males may establish territories and pick on non-spawning females.

BREEDING: Scatters eggs in fine-leaved plants. Not easy to spawn.

TETRA – CHARACIN • PEACEFUL

GLOWLIGHT TETRA *Hemigrammus erythrozonus*

MAXIMUM LENGTH: 1.3 in. (3.3 cm).

NATIVE RANGE: Rio Essequibo, Guyana.

MINIMUM AQUARIUM SIZE: 10 gal. (38 L).

GENERAL SWIMMING LEVEL: Midwater and lower third of tank.

OVERVIEW: The Glowlight Tetra is a perennial favorite among both beginning and advanced aquarists who appreciate the beauty it brings to a tank when kept in schools. This is a small silver tetra adorned with a red "racing stripe," with a gold variety now available.

FEEDING: Omnivore. Glowlight Tetras are greedy eaters that will accept all kinds of commercial aquarium fare, including good-quality flakes, freeze-dried and frozen foods. Supplement their diets with *Spirulina*, and color-enhancing flakes. The occasional feeding of small live foods like adult brine shrimp will also be appreciated.

HABITAT: Dark background and substrate, and plenty of plants with lots of open swimming room is just the ticket for the Glowlight Tetra. Like most tetras, they require good water quality and filtration, as well as regular water changes.

AQUARIUM CARE/BEHAVIOR: Glowlight Tetras are peaceful fishes that should be kept in groups of at least four—the more the merrier. It is slightly larger than the Neon Tetra, and its peaceful disposition makes it an ideal tankmate for a peaceful community aquarium. Keep with fishes of similar size and temperament.

BREEDING: Glowlight Tetras scatter their adhesive eggs among fine-leaved plants, such as *Cabomba*. Most breeders provide them with soft water conditioned with peat moss or peat extract to replicate conditions in their native habitats.

LEMON TETRA *Hyphessobrycon pulchripinnis*

MAXIMUM LENGTH: 1.5 in. (3.8 cm).

NATIVE RANGE: Brazil.

MINIMUM AQUARIUM SIZE: 10 gal. (38 L).

GENERAL SWIMMING LEVEL: Midwater to top.

OVERVIEW: The Lemon Tetra is a subtle beauty, with a translucent body with a faint yellowish tinge. But it is the intense yellow coloration of this fish's anal fin that makes it so popular among tetra enthusiasts and gives it its species name—*pulchripinnis* means "pretty fin." An albino form is also available.

FEEDING: Omnivore. The Lemon Tetra really benefits from color-enhancing foods rich in carotenoids that bring out red and yellow pigments. They are not particularly picky and will devour just about anything offered to them. Provide a varied diet that includes all types of prepared foods like good-quality flakes, as well as freeze-dried, frozen and live foods like *Daphnia* and bloodworms.

HABITAT: An aquarium for the Lemon Tetra should be heavily planted on the sides and back with lots of open areas for the fish to swim in. Dark colors are best for the substrate and background. Susceptible to poor water quality, so regular water changes are a must.

AQUARIUM CARE/BEHAVIOR: Lemon Tetras are a peaceful, schooling fish that are easily maintained in a community tank with other schooling characins of a similar size, as well as other mild-mannered community tankmates. Acquire at least three to make them feel comfortable and allow them to exhibit their natural behaviors.

BREEDING: Lemon Tetras are egg scatterers but are moderately difficult to spawn.

NEON TETRA *Paracheirodon innesi*

MAXIMUM LENGTH: 1 in. (2.5 cm).

NATIVE RANGE: Brazil and Peru, although most commercially bred.

MINIMUM AQUARIUM SIZE: 10 gal. (38 L) long.

GENERAL SWIMMING LEVEL: Midwater to top.

OVERVIEW: Probably the best known tetra and perennially one of the most popular aquarium fishes, the Neon Tetra is a hardy little fish that will usually thrive, even for beginning hobbyists. When kept in large schools in well-planted aquariums, they put on a memorable show. Unlike the Cardinal Tetra (page 132), the broad red band below the neon stripe doesn't extend the entire length of the body, but begins just above the ventral fins and runs into the tail. The blue stripe changes in color as the fish move in and out of the light.

FEEDING: Omnivore. Although the Neon Tetra will accept most aquarium fare, including good-quality flake foods and micro-pellets, it will also need small frozen or live meaty foods, such as brine shrimp or *Daphnia*, to thrive.

HABITAT: The Neon Tetra does not tolerate poor water quality, so place only in a well-established aquarium. They are best kept in a tank well planted on the sides and back with a dark substrate and background.

AQUARIUM CARE/BEHAVIOR: The Neon Tetra is a small, schooling species that does best in groups of at least six (more is better). Because they tend to be timid and are small, avoid keeping them with large or aggressive species that may bully or eat them. Anglefish and Neons, for example, should never be mixed.

BREEDING: Neons are egg scatterers and challenging to breed.

REDEYE TETRA *Arnoldichthys spilopterus*
(African Red-Eyed Characin, Niger Tetra)

MAXIMUM LENGTH: 4 in. (10 cm).

NATIVE RANGE: Tropical West Africa.

MINIMUM AQUARIUM SIZE: 30 gal. (114 L) long.

GENERAL SWIMMING LEVEL: Midwater to top.

OVERVIEW: The Redeye Tetra is an attention-grabbing beauty that is particularly noteworthy for its unusually large silver scales. It is a hardy tetra that is relatively long-lived in the aquarium, but it may nip at the flowing fins of certain other fishes.

FEEDING: Omnivore. The Redeye Tetra prefers small live foods, including brine shrimp and *Daphnia*, but will also accept standard meaty aquarium fare, such as small flakes and granules, as well as freeze-dried and frozen foods. Although primarily a carnivore, it will also benefit from regular offerings of herbivore fare and color-enhancing rations.

HABITAT: Redeye Tetras will need lots of room to swim, so a long tank planted sparsely on the sides and back, with lots of open mid-water swimming space in the center is best. They prefer soft water. Include dark, fine-grade gravel to show off their colors. Any other decor is simply for the benefit of the aquarist.

AQUARIUM CARE/BEHAVIOR: Red-eye Tetras are peaceful schooling fish that should kept in groups of at least three with other fishes of similar temperament. May nip at fishes with long, flowing fins, so avoid such tankmates.

BREEDING: This is a typical egg scatterer that is not difficult to breed in the aquarium.

TETRA – CHARACIN ● PEACEFUL

RUMMYNOSE TETRA *Hemigrammus bleheri*
(Red-Nose Tetra, Firehead Tetra)

MAXIMUM LENGTH: 2 in. (5 cm).

NATIVE RANGE: Brazil and Colombia.

MINIMUM AQUARIUM SIZE: 10 gal. (38 L) long.

GENERAL SWIMMING LEVEL: Midwater.

OVERVIEW: The Rummynose Tetra has a distinctive bright red area around its "nose" that literally glows when the fish is in a good environment. It is often kept with discus because the changing glow of the nose is an early warning sign of water quality problems that would affect the more valuable fish as well. Two similar species are often sold under the same common name—*Hemigrammus rhodostomus* and *Petitella georgiae*.

FEEDING: Omnivore. The Rummynose will accept all types of fine-grade meaty foods, as well as vegetable-based foods. Supplement their diets with occasional feedings of freeze-dried, frozen or live foods, such as brine shrimp or bloodworms. Color-enhancing rations with carotinoids will help keep the red pigments rich and bright.

HABITAT: The Rummynose Tetra is found in clear, shaded blackwater areas in nature. Prefers a darker environment, including substrate and background.

AQUARIUM CARE/BEHAVIOR: The Rummynose Tetra is a peaceful, schooling species that should be kept in groups of at least three, with other small, mild-mannerd fishes like other smallish tetras and *Corydoras* catfishes.

BREEDING: The Rummynose is an egg scatterer that may need soft, peat-steeped water to encourage spawning.

WHITE CLOUD MOUNTAIN FISH *Tanichthys albonubes*

MAXIMUM LENGTH: 1.5 in. (4 cm).

NATIVE RANGE: Southern China, Vietnam.

MINIMUM AQUARIUM SIZE: 20 gal. (76 L).

GENERAL SWIMMING LEVEL: Everywhere, but prefers top.

OVERVIEW: Originally known as the "Poor Man's Neon Tetra," as it was inexpensive and had a similar shape and nice colors. The White Cloud Mountain Fish has an almost reddish-brown body, with a thin silver-green to gold longitudinal line in the middle that runs the length of the body. The tail fin has a bright-red splash of color. There are many commercially developed varieties, including the long-finned "Meteor Minnow" (see image above).

FEEDING: Omnivore. Will accept just about any fine-grade commercial fare, including flakes and pellets, but eagerly consumes small frozen and live foods, such as brine shrimp and *Daphnia*.

HABITAT: It is found among the vegetation of clear mountain streams in the wild, and prefers an aquarium densely planted on the sides and back, with lots of room in the center for swimming and a dark gravel substrate. Provide a layer of floating plants. Although they will adapt to typical tropical aquarium temperatures, they exhibit best coloration in temperatures of 74°F (23.5°C) or less. Can be kept in tanks with no heat, or in outdoor ponds in warmer weather.

AQUARIUM CARE/BEHAVIOR: The White Cloud Mountain Fish is an active schooling species best kept in groups of at least three, or it may become timid and hide out in the corners of the tank. Provide other peaceful, mild-mannered tankmates of similar size.

BREEDING: This is a typical egg scatterer that spawns readily.

WHITE CLOUD – CYPRINID • PEACEFUL

The big, the bad and
the unlikely to survive

The most beguiling, most attractive, most fascinating tropical fishes in the world are now readily available to the freshwater aquarist, who can pick and choose species from the streams, lakes, rivers, sloughs and breeding ponds of Asia, Africa, Latin America, the Australian subcontinent—indeed virtually the entire tropical world.

Not all of these fishes are right for every home aquarium. Many species grow inexorably larger, often rapidly, and it will be up to the aquarist to provide them suitable accommodations to meet their changing needs. If your plans don't include buying a 300-gallon (1,136 L) aquarium any time soon, these are the fish to avoid purchasing in the first place.

Likewise, there are many fish that will cause mayhem in most community aquariums. Keeping aggressive or predatory species is highly attractive to some aquarists, but the tank must be set up correctly and suitable tankmates chosen. For those with peaceful and smaller community species, bringing home a known bully or fisheater can be a painful mistake. There are so many great fish available, it is primarly a matter of knowing what you are buying before you have the fish packed into a plastic bag. While a good fish store will certainly help to steer the hobbyist in the right direction, ultimately, it is up to us, as fishkeepers, to know the profile and needs of the fish—now and as it grows—before we decide to buy.

Some of the fishes listed in this section can, in fact, make good aquarium inhabitants, but only under specific environmental conditions and/or in very large systems. The criteria we use in placing these fishes on a red list include: grows too large for most home aquariums; is highly predatory or territorial and likely to kill and/ or eat other fishes; is hard to feed or has a poor survival record in captivity; is banned in some areas and a threat to local fish populations. Then there are those animals that are a threat to their keepers and that do not make good aquarium animals under any circumstances.

Pacu reaching adult size: an admirable fish, but a nightmare species for hasty purchasers of aquarium livestock. Charming small specimens of an array of commonly sold species can easily outgrow the home aquarium, often leaving the community tank devastated or with a depleted population.

ARCHERFISH (*Toxotes* spp.)

The Archerfishes are interesting, but primarily brackish water species that require a special setup and diet to thrive and are thus not suited for the average tropical community aquarium, where they tend to do poorly and waste away.

SOUTH AMERICAN AROWANA *(Osteoglossum bicirrhosum)*
The South American Arowana is a powerful, large—to almost 4 feet (120 cm)—swimmer that has no place in the average home aquarium. They are also accomplished jumpers and need appropriately large tanks with firmly seated covers.

BICHIR *(Polypterus* spp.*)*
Although appealing when young, many of the African species turn into large, aggressive and predatory fishes with sharp teeth. They are escape artists and have also been known to attack the hands of their owners.

BUCKTOOTH TETRA *(Exodon paradoxus)*
This is an attractive South American fish, but its propensity to prey on small fish and attack larger ones, up to and including Oscars, makes them a poor choice for a community aquarium. Unless kept in large schools, they will also kill each other.

BUTTERFLYFISH *(Pantodon buchholzi)*
Freshwater Butterflyfishes offered for sale are typically not in the best of condition, and they have a poor survival rate in captivity. They feed on live foods taken at the surface and do not do well with most other community residents.

145

BUMBLEBEE GOBY *(Brachygobius spp.)*
Although Bumblebee Gobies are small and attractive fishes, they originate in areas with brackish water and do not do well in fresh-water environments. They are best kept in a brackish-water species aquarium that is fine-tuned to their physiology.

CHACA CATFISH *(Chaca bankanensis)*
This Asian catfish can consume items almost as large as its head, making it a poor choice for the community tank. Also, it has a short dorsal spine that can inflict a painful wound and may exude a slime that kills all other fishes housed with it.

CHINESE ALGAE EATER *(Gyrinocheilus aymonieri)*
Although the Chinese Algae Eater has been in the hobby for decades, these loners grow to about a foot (30 cm) in length and aren't particularly good at eating algae. They get more belligerent and unattractive with age and are a fish to avoid.

CICHLA CICHLIDS *(Cichla* spp.*)*
These South American cichlids get too large for normal aquariums. Also known as Peacock Bass—if you want to know just how big they get, tune in to one of the popular bass fishing shows filmed in their habitats in the wild.

ELECTRIC CATFISH *(Malapterurus spp.)*
Even at a small size, these predatory African catfishes can deliver a powerful shock and have been known to send other fishes housed with them hurtling across the aquarium. The large adult size of most species makes them risky to keep.

ELEPHANTNOSES/BABY WHALES (Family Mormyridae)
While fascinating and highly social, the members of the family Mormyridae have special dietary needs that make them poor candidates for the average community aquarium. Best kept by experienced aquarists in tanks dedicated to this group.

FLAGTAIL PROCHILODUS *(Semaprochilodus insignis)*
Although an eyecatcher when young, the Flagtail Prochilodus soon becomes a large, hyperactive fish that is definitely one of the best jumpers of all the tropical fishes. It can leave a typical communtiy aquarium in ruins.

FOSSIL CAT *(Heteropneustes fossilis)*
Sometimes referred to as the Asian Stinging Catfish, this Asian species is a dangerous fish that can inflict an extremely painful sting, even at small sizes. It is already banned in some states—avoid at all costs.

149

GIANT GOURAMI (*Osphronemus goramy*)
The Giant Gourami is a sedentary, fairly peaceful species that attains lengths of more than 24 in. (60 cm). Although once rare, juveniles are now being imported in large numbers, resulting in many fish being sold to aquarists, who must then deal with them as they grow.

GOLDFISH (*Carassius auratus*)
The Goldfish, in all its many forms, is an excellent aquarium or pond fish, but not for a tropical tank. It is a long-lived coldwater species that will not do well in the warm-water conditions of the average home aquarium.

HALFBEAKS (Family Hemiramphidae)
The Halfbeaks are delicate fishes that are typically nervous aquarium residents and may swim about the tank frantically, often injuring themselves. Add to this their special dietary requirements and you have a group of fishes that are best left to expert aquarists.

IRIDESCENT SHARK (*Pangasianodon hypophthalmus*)
Although usually sold as small individuals, these Asian catfish get far too large—over 4 ft. (130 cm) and some to a whopping 97 pounds (44 kg)—for most home aquariums. With a hyperactive nature, these can be classed, literally, as "tankbusters."

151

MONO *(Monodactylus spp.)*

The various species of Mono are flashy but somewhat timid brackish to marine fishes that get quite large and are easily frightened. They can be expected to do poorly in a standard freshwater community tank setting—better in marine tanks.

MUDSKIPPER *(Periophthalmus spp.)*

Mudskippers are fascinating brackish-water fishes that require a specially set up aquarium to survive. They are worth keeping only if you can offer them a large system that includes both an above-water shoreline and swimming sections.

PACU *(Colossoma spp.)*

Pacus are lovable "Vegetarian Piranhas" that grow humongous (up to 60 pounds; 27.5 kilograms). Most public aquariums do not have room for yet another one of these unfortunate imports; many wind up grilled "on the barbie."

PIKE CICHLIDS *(Crenicichla spp.)*

Pike Cichlids are fascinating South American fishes best left to cichlid specialists. Many get quite large and extremely predatory and, because it is difficult to differentiate between the species, it is often impossible to know what you are getting.

RED-BELLIED PIRANHA *(Pygocentrus nattereri)*
Sale of this piranha is restricted in many states, because of its propensity to eat anything living and the fear that they will impact native species. Although common in many pet stores, they fail to live up to all the excitement and can be boring fish to keep. Definitely not suited for the community aquarium.

PUFFERFISH *(Tetraodon* spp.*)*
Some aquarists make pets of these fishes, but for the most part, puffers are aggressive fishes that are "nippers and biters," and can disrupt a peaceful community aquarium. Consider them specialty fishes best kept in species tanks.

REDTAIL CATFISH *(Phractocephalus hemioliopterus)*
Considered by many to be a "personality" fish, these South American catfish are quite beautiful when small but grow rapidly and reach sizes measured in feet. Most public aquariums don't have room for hobbyist "castoffs." Choose one of its smaller relatives instead.

REEDFISH *(Erpetoichthys calabaricus)*
This West African snake-like fish grows quite large—almost 3 ft. (90 cm) and, because they are able to leave the water for short periods, are known escape artists. Not a good community aquarium fish by any measure.

SCAT *(Scatophagus spp.)*

Scats are brackish to marine species that occasionally move into freshwater. They are generally sold as small juveniles for freshwater aquariums, but may reach sizes up to 15 in. (38 cm) and will require salt levels not typically tolerated by most tropical aquarium species.

SILVER DOLLAR *(Metynnis spp.)*

Most Silver Dollars get quite large, and are active schooling fishes that require very large tanks to thrive. They are not particularly colorful as adults and may eat smaller fishes. Likewise, they are not suited for a planted tank.

SNAKEHEAD *(Channa spp.)*
Snakeheads are large predators that feed on all sorts of animals, including small mammals. They are able to slither out of the water for short periods, making their importation illegal. Prone to jumping out of tanks and will soon outgrow even a 300-gal. (1200 L) tank.

STERLET *(Acipenser ruthenus)*
Sterlets are not tropical species, preferring much colder water temperatures than those offered in a typical community aquarium. Often sold as "dwarf" fishes, they get much larger. Native sturgeon species are banned in many states.

TIGER FISH *(Datnioides* spp.*)*
Although the typical specimens seen in aquarium stores are small and attractive, these Asian fishes become large and greedy predators. Many require brackish water, and are definitely not suitable for a tropical community setting.

TIGER SHOVELNOSE CATFISH *(Pseudoplatystoma* spp.*)*
Although quite popular, these catfishes are highly excitable and often injure themselves when they ram into obstacles in the undersized tanks in which they are typically housed. They grow very large, are predatory and easily "spooked."

SHARK CATFISH *(Hexanematichthys seemanni)*

These are brackish to marine species that will require increasing amounts of salt in the water as they grow. They grow rapidly and become predatory. Even small specimens will rip the scales off other fishes.

WALKING CATFISH *(Clarias spp.)*

The family Clariidae, which includes these African and Asian predatory catfishes, is banned by Federal law because of their ability to "walk" across land areas to get to other waterways when their habitats dry out. They are extremely predatory.

Creating the right menu
for healthy, colorful fishes

In the not-so-distant past, aquarium fish were fed things such as ground puppy biscuits and inferior flake foods composed of the same ingredients, including wheat flour and salt, used in making breakfast cereals and crackers for human consumption.

Today, we know that good nutrition is one of the keys to maintaining a healthy and prosperous aquarium, and providing our charges appropriate foods certainly ranks high on the list of things we need to get right. Fortunately, the foods available to aquarium keepers have improved dramatically in recent years and it is not hard to keep our fishes well-fed and thriving.

To the uninitiated, the idea of feeding aquarium fish can seem pretty simple: once a day, you open a container of fish food, sprinkle a pinch or two on top of the water and watch the fish swim up to eat. Job finished...right?

To do things right and to see your aquarium fishes at their best and most colorful, perhaps even witness spawning behaviors, there is a bit more involved. Like most forms of life (humans included), fishes need a varied and balanced diet that provides for all their nutritional needs. Protein, carbohydrates, lipids (fats), vitamins and minerals are just some of the components that make up a good diet.

Some credit a young German scientist, Dr. Ulrich Baensch, with revolutionizing the aquarium hobby in the 1950s when he developed flake foods formulated to meet the needs of captive fishes. Prior to this, aquarists relied on hard-to-supply live foods caught in local streams and ponds or on pulverized cereal products and foods for other animals. Flake foods helped bring aquarium keeping within the reach of millions more people, but for decades the quality of such rations varied wildly, with many more appropriate for a pet chicken than animals of aquatic origin.

Luckily for aquarists, today there are so many generally excellent prepared foods to choose from that we can easily match the foods to the types of fishes we keep. In place of the heavy doses of

Group of robust Platies display vibrant colors that come with proper feeding.

161

wheat flour, the better new foods are rich in fish meal, shrimp meal, krill, fish roe, vitamins, minerals and color-enhancing pigments. Cheap fillers from the bakery industry have moved down the ingredient list in all of the best fish foods.

In addition to well-balanced community-type tropical foods, there is also an increasing variety of specialty, or species-specific, foods such as "herbivore" and "carnivore" diets. There are even foods aimed at a particular fish or group of fishes—betta, cichlid or catfish diets. Then there are the different styles of food to choose from—flakes, discs, pellets, granules of all sizes, sticks, sinking wafers and so on, as well as freeze-dried, frozen and, yes, live.

In fact, if you are new to feeding fishes and try to browse the shelves of a well-stocked aquarium store, you may be overwhelmed by the sheer number and variety on display. There is no need to let all this go to your head. Feeding most of the species in this book is not difficult. The bottom line here, and an open secret, is that most of the foods you see in good aquarium stores will work reasonably well for most commonly kept aquarium fish. The important thing is to provide a variety of different foods. It is possible to feed a community tank with one well-balanced ration, but your fishes will do better if you vary their diets. (Your role as a fishkeeper will also be more interesting and rewarding.)

SETTING UP YOUR FISH FOOD PANTRY

So, where to start? While some fish do have special dietary needs that must be taken into account, the nutritional requirements of the great majority of tropical fishes are easily met by providing a varied diet of standard prepared aquarium rations, regularly supplemented with specialty items, such as "meaty" foods or those that are vegetable-based.

A well-stocked fish food pantry will include at least a couple of types of flake foods. There are, of course, the basic rations, typically sold as "tropical flakes," which are good for most tropical aquarium fishes. Then there are the vegetable-based flakes, which are richer in vegetable matter and usually contain Spirulina algae. Both of these varieties should be included in your pantry. The idea of providing an assortment of foods is based on the fact that, no matter how good a particular food is, there is always the possibility that it may be lack-

*Redtailed Black Shark (*Epalzeorhynchos bicolor) *grazing. The modern aquarist can easily provide a nutritious and varied diet to all species commonly kept.*

ing in some of the nutrients essential to the well-being of the fish you are keeping. Also, "variety is the spice of life," even where your fish are concerned. Will they be able to live and even thrive on a diet consisting of just one type of food? Probably...but would they be a bit happier with a variety of foods in their lives? I think so.

Depending on the type of fish you are keeping, you may also want to include one of the "sinking" varieties. In a tank with mostly surface or mid-water swimming (and eating) fishes, it may be difficult for sufficient amounts of food to reach the lower levels of the aquarium, where a number of species, such as the catfishes, spend most of their lives. While some bottom dwellers may quickly learn to come up to the surface for food, others may not be quick learners or have the ability to do so. The styles of foods you choose should take into account the types of fishes you keep.

When it comes to prepared foods, it is best not to purchase too large a quantity at one time. Once opened (and, in some cases, even before), fish foods are subject to nutritional breakdown. Think of a box of breakfast cereal. Within a few weeks, if not eaten, it loses its crunch, takes on a rancid taste and loses its palatability.

The vitamin content also suffers. Purchasing smaller containers will allow you to restock your pantry on a regular basis, thereby helping to guarantee good nutritional content of what you are offer-

Anatomically designed to feed from the surface, the Silver Hatchetfish exemplifies species that need special attention to ensure they get enough to eat.

ing. (Bulk fish foods, exposed to the open air, are shunned by most advanced hobbyists.)

TYPICAL "MEATY" FOODS

The regular feeding of some types of meaty items should be considered essential unless you are keeping a strictly herbivorous community or species. Offering these foods at least five to seven times a week will go a long way toward promoting fish vitality and health. Many of the commonly available meaty foods come in a number of forms: frozen, freeze-dried and live.

Brine Shrimp (*Artemia salina*) is a standard food in the aquarium hobby and it comes in a variety of forms, including frozen, freeze-dried and live. Brine shrimp are aquatic crustaceans famously harvested in San Francisco Bay and the Great Salt Lake, but also in other bays and estuaries worldwide. This prolific little animal has the ability to produce egglike cysts that can survive for years in a dry state before hatching within hours after being returned to saltwater. (These are the sea monkeys you might have bought as a youngster.)

While brine shrimp are by no means the most nutritionally complete food, they are still a good addition to an overall dietary profile for many fish. Depending on the need, they may be enriched before feeding with one of the many vitamin supplements, such as Selco™ . (Or, in the case of commercial brands, before freezing.) When feeding the frozen variety, it is best to take the desired amount and let it melt in a container of tap water. (This would be your fish-only feeding container.) The shrimp can then be poured into a fine mesh net and rinsed well under running tap water of approximate aquarium water temperature to avoid adding unneeded pollutants to the tank.

These can then be fed to your fish in small amounts to make sure everything is eaten. You could also add the shrimp in with some flake food. The important thing to remember is not to add the frozen shrimp without first thawing and rinsing. Once you've seen the murky fluid and sediments that escape when you add a frozen piece directly into the aquarium, you'll think twice before doing so again.

Freeze-dried brine shrimp is also available and should be treated the same as the frozen variety. The cubes, or chunks, can be broken up and put into a container of water. You can gently press them with your fingers to help them absorb water (re-hydrate). Then rinse and feed to the fish.

Many stores may also carry live brine shrimp, typically available in set portions. Feeding these can add another level of feeding enjoyment to your fishes by stimulating their prey capture response—they get to hunt the shrimp just as they would pursue live items in the wild. Do not add the water brine shrimp come in to your tank, as it has a high salt content. Treat as with the frozen and freeze-dried varieties.

Bloodworms are the larvae of midge-type flying insects and are relished by practically all tropical fish. Both frozen and freeze-dried varieties are available, and should be served using the same procedure described for brine shrimp. Bloodworms are an excellent food source and should be considered a necessary part of any good tropical fish diet. A word of caution here—some hobbyists are allergic to bloodworms and may develop a rash after coming in contact with them. The frozen chunks can be broken off in the package and added to the thawing container without having to touch them.

Krill or euphausids are shrimp-like marine crustaceans that make an excellent food for tropical fish. Krill are typically available in at least three different sizes, the smallest of which is usually sold as "plankton" and seems to be the size of choice for most fishes. Larger krill can be used in feeding big carnivorous fishes. Again, the frozen and freeze-dried varieties are the most commonly available.

Of course, brine shrimp, bloodworms and krill are not the only live foods available. There are also white worms, black worms, *Daphnia*, glass worms (an insect larvae) and *Cyclops*, among others. Your local store can help you in deciding which ones to choose.

There are also an increasing number of frozen food mixtures available. These incorporate a variety of foods into an-easy-to-feed mixture, and are usually supplemented with vitamins and minerals. These foods are often targeted for specific groups of fishes (e.g. "cichlid formula"), but are generally a good additional food source for most fishes. Again, the "thawing and rinsing principle" applies here.

FEEDING THE "VEGETARIAN" FISH

In these enlightened times, we must not forget the veggie lovers. While most tropical fish will benefit from having some vegetable material in their diets, there are those, such as the pleco-type catfishes (i.e., *Otocinclus* spp., *Ancistrus* spp.), that feed primarily on green matter in nature, and for whom vegetable-based foods are essential.

Flake foods that are high in vegetable material are very good for them, but may often be eaten by faster, surface and mid-water fishes before reaching the fish that truly need them. There are some commonly available vegetable-based foods designed specifically for the groups of fishes that are more compact, and heavier, including discs and wafers, that sink quickly to the bottom. Most of these fishes have rasping-type teeth that will make quick work of these foods.

There are also algae-based frozen foods, marketed mainly for marine fishes, that make ideal plant-based meals for these freshwater fishes. (As always with frozen fish foods, don't forget to "thaw and rinse" to avoid polluting your tank.)

Finally, the use of fresh, or even some canned, vegetables as a supplemental food source should not be overlooked and will be appreciated by many fishes...even some that might surprise you. Darker leafy vegetables, such as Romaine lettuce, leaf-type lettuce, and spinach, are eagerly eaten by many fishes (avoid lighter colored

*Algae-eating catfishes such as this Royal Pleco (*Panaque nigrolineatus*) juvenile often get neglected by aquarists who assume they can fend for themselves. Appropriate rations are now available for the plecos and other bottom feeders.*

lettuce like heads of iceberg, which is mostly water and cellulose).

Leafy greens are a good choice not only for pleco and other catfishes, but cichlids and a variety of other fishes may also eagerly consume these foods. Be sure to rinse the lettuce or spinach leaves thoroughly under running tap water and then add them to the tank (one leaf at a time is ideal). Because lettuce leaves float, they will need to be secured so that bottom feeders have access to them. There are special clips sold in aquarium stores just for this purpose. You can also use clean, washed rubber bands to attach the leaves to tank decor (rocks, driftwood, etc.) or pieces of stone.

Many frozen, or canned, vegetables, packed in water, can also be used and are relished by plecos, as well as other fishes. Green beans (regular or French-cut) are especially appreciated. Again, rinse well and then add them to the tank in small amounts to make sure all is eaten. This is an area where you can experiment, always remembering to use small quantities in case your fish might not like a particular item. As with other foods, after a short period of time uneaten amounts should be removed from the aquarium.

Fishes with red and yellow pigments, such as this attractive male Platy, can benefit greatly from regular feedings of a good color-enhancing ration.

COLOR-ENHANCING FOODS

A growing trend in formulating better tropical fish foods is the inclusion of color-enhancing supplements. Of particular interest are the carotenoid pigments (including carotenes and xanthophylls), which can strengthen and enhance the natural colors of the fishes eating them. The colors most commonly affected by these substances are the reds and yellows, but blues, greens and other colors will also show improvement.

It is a good idea to add at least one such food to your basic fish food pantry. You can choose the style of food depending on the fishes you are maintaining. For example, if you are keeping primarily smaller fishes, a flake formula will generally suffice. But, if you havelarger fishes, you might want to consider an appropriate pellet or stick-style food. Just be sure to remember that all fishes can eat smaller foods, while only larger fishes will be able to easily take the larger varieties. Again, when feeding these color-enhancing foods, you want to make sure that all the fishes in your tank are getting their fair share.

HOW AND WHEN TO FEED

In the wild, most fish feed naturally throughout the day—or during dark hours if they are nocturnal. In the aquarium, as food is offered, they will eat their fill. For the most part, it is not common for most fish in the wild to consume only one large meal a day. It is actually quite difficult to overfeed most fish, as they tend to stop eating or at least slow down once they are full. Overwhelming the tank's waste-handling capacities with uneaten food is an easy matter.

A good rule of thumb is to feed your fishes three to four smaller meals a day. No uneaten food should remain after five minutes or so. The spacing of these meals may depend on the fishes being kept and the schedule of the keeper. It doesn't take long to feed the tank, and it is a perfect time to be able to take a look and make sure that all the fishes are doing and eating well. Again, you can mix and match foods, feeding some flakes and bloodworms one time, and brine shrimp and lettuce the next. In fact, this undoubtedly mimics a more natural feeding process.

If you are keeping nocturnal or timid fishes, be sure to offer them food about a half hour or so after the lights are turned off at night, when the feeding response of the other fishes is reduced. Use some of the sinking varieties or even fresh or canned vegetables. This will help guarantee them their fair share of food. It's also a good idea to offer food the first thing in the morning when the lights are turned on.

Predatory species may be able to survive on one large meal, but in the typical community setting, they will simply consume the regular succession of smaller portions offered. Even if you have a large pet fish, such as an Oscar, it is probably not a good idea to offer its entire daily ration at one fell swoop. Feeding aquarium fishes is actually quite simple. With a little thought and planning, everything else will fall into place and your fish will be happy and healthy.

Preventing and stopping common fish diseases

Mary E. Sweeney

Much of the time disease in the aquarium is, not to put too fine a point on it, a disaster. The trouble starts with a new fish or fishes being introduced to the established aquarium. The next thing, there's a spritzing of spots or a tilting fish, and before you know it, the population starts to decline. Without appropriate intervention, the more delicate fishes are all dead, and before long, the hardier fishes are gone as well. What's to be done?

FIRST AND FOREMOST...

This cannot be emphasized strongly enough nor often enough: quarantine all new fishes before introducing them into your healthy aquarium. How many piscine souls could have been saved throughout fishkeeping history if only we could drill this into our heads! (I could not say this so emphatically had I not had so much personal experience over the years...) By keeping new fishes in a separate tank for even as little as a week—although 30 days is highly recommended—you can avoid spreading virtually all of the contagious diseases to the fishes you already have. Also, it's easier to treat diseases, whether they occur in your home aquarium or in a new acquisition, in the unadorned quarantine tank. Think about it the next time you're planning a fish purchase.

When treating your sick fish, the quarantine tank becomes the hospital tank. It is difficult and often impossible to successfully treat fishes in a show tank. Concerns over filter bacteria viability, plants and medication use, disease vectors in the aquarium, gallonage, and many other variables, even to the amount of mulm in the substrate, make it risky to use medications in the community aquarium. It is far more effective, when treating fishes, to use a simple temporary setup. You can use a small aquarium (whether a clean, fish-only bucket, plastic storage container) of perhaps 10 gallons—depending

Overcrowding is a surefire route to stressing tropical fishes and allowing the onset of various health problems caused by parasites and poor water quality.

A quarantine tank can double as a hospital tank where sick fish can be treated without introducing potent medications into the display aquarium. An inexpensive 10-gallon tank with heater, thermometer, sponge filter and synthetic plants and/or hiding places are the only requirements. Salt is often a useful remedy.

on the size and number of fishes to be treated—a heater, thermometer, and a sponge filter with perhaps an extra airstone. Nothing else is really required except some cover for the fish to hide in, under, or behind, as is their nature. Different strokes for different species. The vertical plastic plants that make an angelfish feel invisible would translate into the underside of a log for a pleco or a rocky cave for an mbuna. If you must treat the fishes in the show tank, start with a 50% water change, clean the gravel very well, and increase aeration before proceeding with carefully selected medications.

Be willing to accept success at any point in the process. If, after performing the water changes and adding salt, the fish are not as skittish or their color has improved, consider that this has altered the course of the disease process and be willing to abandon the use of antibiotics, dyes, or other chemicals.

Salt is an extremely effective curative in the freshwater aquarium. I don't believe that freshwater fishes should be kept in salted water, unless they are truly brackish-water fishes, and certainly there are some fishes, generally scaleless, that don't respond well to salt, medications, or dyes, but these exceptions aside, common salt used as a dip or a bath is often enough to eliminate the need for further medication. It is known to destroy many kinds of bacteria, to increase slime-coat production (a positive thing), and even to cause some parasites to drop off. It can also serve as an all-round tonic, but do not mistake that for a reason to keep freshwater fishes in a constantly salt-enhanced aquarium.

This brings us to another point on the health-disease continuum in the aquarium. Fish often react to incorrect temperatures, out-of-whack pH or alkalinity, poor lighting, wrong or insufficient foods, hostile tankmates, bad water chemistry, and certain other unnatural conditions in one simple way: they get sick.

THE STRESS FACTOR

The most frequent cause of fish loss is not disease as such, but stress. While we may not have much sympathy for the overachiever who complains of their own self-induced stress, the fishes we adopt into our homes are at our tender mercies. We must be alert to stressors in their environment if we are to keep them healthy. The aquarium should be placed in a quiet area so the fishes are not constantly bombarded by human activities. All of the fishes must be compatible. If a fish is constantly being chased, it will surely die. It may not die from wounds inflicted by the other fish, but the stress of being pursued will diminish not only its standard of living but the duration as well.

Water chemistry, quality, and temperature must also all be

WAYS TO REDUCE STRESS
IN YOUR AQUARIUM

- **Select the species** you keep carefully—not all species deal with stress in the same way.
- **Feed your fish** a nutritious diet.
- **Select tankmates** carefully to help avoid aggression problems.
- **Provide plenty** of hiding places.
- **Maintain optimaL** environmental conditions (good water quality, steady temperature, regular lighting cycles).
- **Reduce the liklihood** of sudden changes in environmental conditions.
- **Capturing, moving or handling** your fish should be done as infrequently as possible.

within normal limits or the fish will be stressed and stress will eventually kill them outright or set them up for the various disease processes that will eventually do them in. There are many sources of stress in the life of a fish, from being chased by a net to people tapping on the glass of the aquarium. If the fish hides or flees constantly, we can be fairly certain it is highly stressed. If the fish are trying to escape from the water onto dry land, you can form your own conclusions.

WATER QUALITY

Polluted aquarium water is a certain cause of disease. Toxins in the water kill fish. Rotting plants, excess food, and fish waste all pollute the water. Dead fish definitely pollute the water. Polluted water is full of bacteria and fungus that will be happy to move uptown from their homes on fish waste to reside on the fish itself. Such is the cycle of life and death in the aquarium. When the aquarist becomes complacent and the partial water changes become less frequent, the stage is set for various diseases to show up in the tank. The simple act of adding another fish—even a healthy fish—can alter the delicate balances of the aquarium, and there's your next disease outbreak. Regular water testing is essential to maintaining high water quality.

When ammonia, nitrite, nitrate, or phosphate levels begin to rise, there are several remedies. More frequent and larger changes with pure aged water should be performed. Larger than normal water changes in the 25-50 percent range are necessary as otherwise the dilution and removal of these nutrients is negligible and the problem lingers or becomes worse. If you are feeding more than your fishes are eating, it may also be time to use some restraint or think about more efficient filtration. Try hand-feeding your fishes for a while to monitor the quantity of food.

AMMONIA LEVELS

In the case of high ammonia levels—and ammonia is highly toxic to fishes, with some simply being more hardy, but none immune to the effect—reducing the ammonia level with water changes and the use of zeolite in the filter will help tremendously. The signs of ammonia poisoning are flashing (rubbing the irritated body and gills on surfaces in the aquarium) and rapid breathing in the initial stages, and as the ammonia levels increase, lethargy, loss of appetite, laying on the bottom with clamped fins, or gasping at the water surface if the gills have been affected.

At high levels (>0.1 mg/liter NH_3) even relatively short exposures can lead to skin, eye, and gill damage. An immediate water change is called for. Adding an airstone and one teaspoon of salt per gallon of water, provided there are no delicate plants in the

A rather pathetic-looking little Dwarf Suckermouth Catfish, emaciated, with poor color and deteriorating fins. Bringing such a fish home from the pet store is often the precursor to major disease outbreaks.

aquarium, will work as an emergency stopgap until you are able to change enough water to reduce the nitrite to a safe level. If water changes have been neglected for some time, and conditions are dreary in the aquarium, it is better to use a combination of water changes and ammonia, nitrate, and phosphate resins plus carbon plus biofiltration to bring the tank back to a healthful state rather than to rely on huge, potentially shocking, water changes with raw tapwater.

PARASITES

Ich, velvet, and skin and gill flukes are among the more common parasites that live on the outside of the fishes. These enemies can be treated with good success provided they are caught early and treated appropriately.

Ich and velvet both show up as spots, with ich being white and velvet looking like golden dust. With both diseases, the fish flash frequently and seem to be in acute discomfort. Often, by the time you notice the spots, the parasites are already quite heavy on the fish. The few spots on day one may have increased to a heavy coat by day three. Also, there will be parasites on the gills as well, and the delicate gill filaments you cannot see are often in bad shape while just a few external spots are apparent on the tail and fins of the fish.

For virtually any parasite, you are treating both fish and tank. Even if you use a hospital tank, you must treat the evacuated show tank as well. Start with a major water change and gravel vacuuming to reduce the parasite population, then raise the temperature slowly to 88 to 90°F (31 to 32°C). After three weeks, all the parasites will have hatched and died off in the empty aquarium. Bring the temperature back down to normal, then introduce one test fish and observe.

Often, in addition to heat and a water change, the only other medication required is one teaspoon per gallon of salt. Besides stimulating slime coat production, the salt kills the free-swimming parasites, which will stop the infestation in its tracks, provided the treatment is carried out for the necessary length of time: 21 days. If further medication is needed, malachite green and formalin combinations are very effective.

For velvet infestations, the same treatment of hygiene/aeration/heat/salt as above is highly recommended, but if medication is required, acriflavine, used according to manufacturer's instructions will clear up any residual infestation.

Gill and skin flukes present with similar symptoms of labored breathing and flashing, and breeders will find that their fry will die off a few a days after hovering at the waterline gasping for air. Again, hygiene is a huge part of the treatment; as with any outbreak of disease, start with the water changes. Heavy fluke infestations affecting more than one fish are usually caused by overcrowding, poor water quality, or water with a high organic content. Under these ideal circumstances for pests, parasites multiply rapidly. Again, the hygiene and salt bath regimen is exceptionally valuable. Malachite green and formalin, used according to manufacturer's directions, will generally help cope with heavy infestations.

BACTERIAL INFECTIONS

Bacteria are everywhere, the good ones, the bad, and the indifferent. Our problems with bacteria in the aquarium are virtually always associated with overfeeding, overcrowding, and poor water quality. Some bacteria show up in the form of fin and tail rot. Other times, the fish's eyes will bulge from their sockets, and sometimes the bellies of the fish will swell until the scales pop out like pinecones. Some of these bacterial conditions can be treated, some not. Often, the odds are only as good as a roll of the dice, but it is very satisfying when a fish that was very sick recovers and goes on to a long life in the aquarium.

Fin and tail rot, open wounds, fungus, pop-eye, dropsy, and many other similar infections do need antibiotics. As it is difficult for most of us to determine which medication is ideal for which disease, manufacturers offer broad-spectrum antibiotics and indicate on the packaging which symptoms the medication is useful against. Consult the packaging for similarity of symptoms. Also, aquarium pharmaceutical companies generally provide support numbers. Avail yourself of the advice of the experienced.

Don't let fish diseases get you down. Sometimes fish die for no apparent reason. Take heed, and quarantine!

Modes of reproduction in tropical aquarium fishes

For many freshwater aquarists, one of the joys of keeping exotic fishes is to encourage and witness the reproductive lives of their fishes. Unlike many marine species, which can be challenging to spawn in home-scale aquariums and which often produce exceedingly tiny, hard-to-feed larvae, many freshwater species are not especially difficult to breed. In fact, in many cases, such as the livebearers and cichlids, it may be virtually impossible to keep the fish from doing what comes naturally.

Aside from the satisfaction that breeding your aquarium residents provides, there are a variety of other motivations. Some enthusiasts are able to support their hobby by offering the progeny of favorite fishes for sale to other aquarists or local aquarium stores. Still others breed their fishes to witness the incredible repertoire of interesting behaviors associated with courtship, spawning and fry rearing exhibited by a wide array of fishes, such as the cichlids. And finally, there are those who breed their fishes in search of the "perfect" specimen to display at various fish shows.

As with all living things, breeding is about nothing less than the survival of the species. To that end, freshwater fishes have developed a number of strategies to assist them in this effort. Most freshwater fish reproduce sexually, and can be divided into two main categories, based on their reproductive styles: those that give birth to live offspring and those that lay eggs. With the first group, the reproductive process is more-or-less simple and straightforward, although there are instances where the process is a bit more complicated. Among the egg layers, however, the variety seen in their reproductive strategies is astonishing at times. At the simplest level, there are those that release eggs and sperm directly into the water where they are fertilized and fall to the bottom (or in some cases rise to the surface), or those that deposit their eggs on some type of substrate. There are also those that brood the eggs in their mouths. Here is a brief introduction to the modes of reproduction you may witness in your aquarium.

Reproduction happens: Firemouth Cichlid guarding its brood of young.

LIVEBEARERS

The livebearers, most famously the guppy, mollies, platies and swordtails, produce eggs that are fertilized and then develop internally in the female until she delivers fully developed baby livebearers after a brief period. The male livebearer fertilizes the eggs by using his modified anal fin, called a gonopodium, to deliver his sperm directly into the female's reproductive canal.

Livebearers practice no parental care and the fry are basically left to their own devices and are at the mercy of the elements. If special precautions are not taken in the closed confines of an aquarium, most of these tiny livebearers will become food for the other tank inhabitants, including their parents, which are often first in line at the buffet. In the wild, a similar situation occurs, although the chances of more fry surviving are somewhat better just by virtue of the fact that there are more areas for them to find refuge. The aquarist wishing to raise the fry must remove them to a separate rearing tank to prevent their being eaten or isolate the gravid female in a breeding trap or a heavily planted aquarium.

Curiously, many female livebearers are able to store sperm internally and use it to fertilize additional batches of eggs over a period of several months. It isn't unusual for a female guppy, for instance, to give birth to baby guppies even though there are no other guppies in the tank!

THE EGG LAYERS

In this mode of reproduction, for the most part, the eggs and sperm are released into the water where fertilization then takes place. There are, as you might expect, many variations on this theme. In some species, such as the South American Zamora Catfish, the eggs are internally fertilized before they are deposited.

In the egg scatterers, the process is so quick that it is often over before you know what has happened. Female egg scatterers release their eggs into the open water, usually at the mid-water to top levels of the tank, with the male releasing a cloud of sperm at the same time—the eggs are fertilized and their job is done. The eggs drift up into floating plants or down among pebbles, rocks and grasses. Some eggs remain loose, while others are adhesive and designed to cling to plants until hatching. The egg scatterers typically practice no

Geophagus steindachneri *is one of the South American "eartheater" cichlids that practice maternal mouthbrooding, with the female caring for her young.*

parental care and the pair quickly join the other inhabitants of the tank by feasting on their progeny.

Hobbyists who wish to breed these fishes will need to take precautions to protect the eggs. Success means setting up a separate breeding tank and then removing the pair once the eggs are scattered. But sometimes in a heavily planted community tank, some of these tiny fry may escape predation and be seen hiding among the plants or in a crevice. This is always a thrill.

Some egg layers are a little more selective and deliberately deposit their eggs on or in a particular site. The popular Corydoras catfishes will place their larger adhesive eggs either singly or in groups on plants or aquarium equipment or glass. Other egg layers display more complex methods of reproduction. In many substrate-spawning cichlids, male and female form a strong pair bond and will lay and fertilize their eggs in a protected area and then defend them against all comers (including the aquarist's hand or a net).

MOUTHBROODERS

Other cichlids, a number of anabantids, and even some catfishes, practice mouthbrooding, in which the eggs are picked up and carried in the mouth of one, or both, parents after spawning. There is a great degree of variation in this reproductive style. Most familiar to aquarists are the maternal mouthbrooders. All Lake Malawi cichlids typically seen in the hobby practice this style of breeding. The females pick up the eggs, which may be fertilized externally or in her mouth, and keep them in their mouths until the young fish are fully developed. In many species, the fry will continue to return (or at least try to do so) to the female's mouth for protection even after they are completely developed. In a few other species, the male broods the eggs and in yet others, both parents share the egg-holding duties by passing them back and forth. Most of the mouthbrooders practice some form of parental care after the fry are hatched.

BUBBLENEST BUILDERS

Nest building is also seen in quite a number of fishes, most notable among these being bettas and gouramis, which create bubblenests. These nests are produced by the male using special secretions to extend the life of the bubbles he produces. This is an on-going process and once the male is in a nest-building mode, he will continually repair the nest and add new bubbles. Often, small amounts of plant material, also gathered by the male, will be incorporated into the nest to help hold it together. Once the male has constructed the nest, he will begin courting a female and spawning will take place. The male then gathers the eggs and places them in among the nesting materials (bubbles and plants). Once spawning is completed, the female should be removed from the tank, as the male will view her as a threat to "his" eggs.

FEEDING THE FRY

Most livebearer babies and the released young of mouthbrooding cichlids, for example, are large enough to accept flake foods run through a coffee grinder (dedicated for just this use) until they are extremely fine as a good first food. There are also a number of commercial liquid and fine flake fry foods available for just this purpose. These can be supplemented with some meaty foods, such as newly hatched brine shrimp (*Artemia* nauplii).

The fry of most egg layers will not need to be fed until they are free swimming, as they will continue to feed on an attached egg sac until it is used up. The initial free-swimming fry are quite

Betta beneath its nest of sticky bubbles and bits of floating plant material.

small and will require correspondingly small foods. Again, there are a number of liquid and fine flake fry foods that will do quite well. Some aquarists may want to culture their own foods, such as "green water" (unicellular algae produced by placing a jar of fertilized water in a sunny spot) or "Infusoria" (microorganisms and algae that develop from rotting vegetable or plant matter, again, in a separate container). Even bits of hard-boiled egg yolk can be offered. Again, most of these foods are also available in commercial versions. Many of these foods can quickly foul the water. Remember to pay careful attention to water quality in the fry-rearing tank and remove any uneaten or rotting foods.

SCIENTIFIC NAME INDEX

[SPECIES TO AVOID IN RED]

184

SCIENTIFIC NAME INDEX

[SPECIES TO AVOID IN RED]

SCIENTIFIC NAME INDEX

[SPECIES TO AVOID IN RED]

SCIENTIFIC NAME INDEX

[SPECIES TO AVOID IN RED]

COMMON NAME INDEX

[SPECIES TO AVOID IN RED]

COMMON NAME INDEX

COMMON NAME INDEX

[SPECIES TO AVOID IN RED]

CREDITS

PHOTOGRAPHY:
Principal Photographer: **Aaron Norman**
Pages 25, 48, 50, 51, 52, 53, 55, 56, 57, 62, 63, 70, 76, 79, 83, 94, 107, 110, 115, 116, 117, 136, 148, 150, 151, 154, 159

Claro Cortes IV/Reuters/Corbis, page 102
Johnny Jensen, page 58
Kris Gammill, page 154 (bottom)

All other images from the
T.F.H. Publications Archives
Including the work of:
Dr. Gerald R. Allen, Takashi Amano, M. Brichard, Theirry Brichard, J. Elias, A. Kochetov, Ad Konigs, Horst Linke, Oliver Lucanus, Ken Lucas, M.P. & C. Piednor, Edward Taylor, Andre Roth, Mark Smith and others.

DESIGN: Linda Provost

COLOR: Digital Engine

ILLUSTRATION: Joshua Highter

EDITING: James M. Lawrence, Judith Billard, Alesia Depot, Janice Heilmann, Scott W. Michael, John Sweeney, Mary E. Sweeney

Contribute your comments and suggestions for future editions of this book:
editors@microcosmaquariumexplorer.com
www.MicrocosmAquariumExplorer.com

Kathleen Wood has been involved in the keeping of tropical fishes for more than 30 years. She served as editor of *Aquarium Fish* Magazine for many years and was instrumental in establishing and editing *Aquarium USA*, *Marine Fish & Reef USA*, and *Koi World*. She is currently the head of editorial operations for *Coral* Magazine, the English-language edition of the German publication *Koralle*. Kathleen is active in a number of conservation projects and animal welfare pursuits. She lives with a menagerie that includes her two bulldogs, a lab, several cats, an Oscar tank and a 150-gallon above-ground pond with goldfish in Laguna Beach, California.

Scott W. Michael is a marine biologist, lifelong fishkeeper and a former aquarium retail store owner. He is the author of the best-selling *PocketExpert Guides to Marine Fishes* and *Reef Aquarium Fishes*, as well as *The Adventurous Aquarist Guide to Saltwater Fishes*. He lives in Lincoln, Nebraska with his wife Janine.

Mary E. Sweeney is the former editor of *Tropical Fish Hobbyist* Magazine and a longtime book author and editor who worked for many years with the Axelrod family and T.F.H. Publications in Neptune City, New Jersey. She lives, writes and keeps tropical fishes at the Water Witch Club, her family home in Monmouth Hills, New Jersey.